CW01666758

THE NEWCASTLE UNITED STORY

AN OFFICIAL HISTORY OF NEWCASTLE UNITED FOOTBALL CLUB

PAUL JOANNOU

g

Lomond Books
A Grange Publication

© 1999

Published by Grange Communications Ltd., Edinburgh, under licence from Newcastle United Football Company.

Printed in the EU.

Photographs and illustrations are courtesy of Newcastle United F.C., Ian Horrocks and the Paul Joannou Collection.
Many of the photographs reproduced are from original material in the archives at Newcastle United F.C., who also retain the rights to official photocall pictures from the modern era taken by the appointed Club Photographer. Most remaining photographs are from the private collection of the author. We have been unable to trace the sources of all these pictures, but any photographer involved is invited to contact the publishers in writing providing proof of copyright.

ISBN: 1-84204-007-3

Whilst every effort has been made to ensure the accuracy of information contained within this book, the publishers cannot be held responsible for any errors or omissions.

Views expressed are those of the author and do not necessarily represent those of the publishers or the football club.

All rights reserved. This book is sold subject to the condition that it may not be reproduced, stored in a retrieval system, or transmitted, in any form or by any means, electronic, mechanical, photocopying, recording or otherwise without the publishers' prior consent.

CONTENTS

INTRODUCTION

As football enters the new century, the game in Britain has changed dramatically. A group of powerful, super-rich clubs are beginning to dominate the sport which is developing into a highly lucrative, professional and prestigious business. Newcastle United Football Club is one of those clubs.

With a proud history and tradition as one of football's elite, the Magpies have been transformed from an ailing and near bankrupt club at the start of the nineties, into an organisation ranked not only one of the biggest in this country but in the whole world. The vision and business acumen of Sir John Hall during that period has given Tyneside a club that is able to move into the new century as a major force.

Newcastle United's history is packed with incident and drama, from the days on Victorian Tyneside when pioneer clubs Newcastle East End and Newcastle West End started kicking a ball around. There have been many triumphs, as well as tragedies, and many moments of controversy on and off the field which have kept United as one of the game's headliners.

They were Edwardian England's top side and one of the best teams around during the inter-war period. The boom years that followed peace saw United at centre stage, with three Wembley victories in only five years. Then, on to European glory and more Wembley drama before a decade of incident which led to the remarkable resurgence and the side branded The Entertainers. Newcastle United finished twice as runners-up in the Premiership and twice as runners-up in the Wembley showpiece of the FA Cup final as the Millennium approached.

Famous names galore have pulled on the black 'n' white striped shirt in over a century of action. Names like Gallacher, Milburn, Macdonald and recent personalities Keegan, Waddle, Beardsley, Gazza and Alan Shearer, only a few of a whole line of larger than life characters to have worn the famous shirt. Recently the Magpies have been led by some of football's biggest names too; Ossie Ardiles, Kevin Keegan, Kenny Dalglish and Ruud Gullit – four celebrated stars from the world stage. Now ex-England manager, Bobby Robson, has taken the reins.

With a modern stadium to house a loyal and fervent support matched by few, Newcastle United is one of the country's superclubs. This history will give supporters an introduction to the Magpies' colourful past and present.

MODERN MAGPIES

As Newcastle United enter the new Millennium, the club is one of the biggest and most powerful around, now a European giant. The transformation of the Magpies during the nineties decade has been staggering. At the start of the era Newcastle was a club in rapid decline. The black'n'whites were struggling to make an impact on the old Division Two. They had a meagre turnover of around £4m, were deep in debt and with a stadium in need of much redevelopment.

That has all changed. As the Magpies face the first season of the 21st century, United are a Premier League force having achieved two runners-up spots in the Title race and having reached two FA Cup finals in succession. Turnover of the club is one now one of the largest in the world, approaching £45m. St James Park has been transformed at a huge cost and will cater for 51,000 supporters in spectacular surroundings.

Back at the start of the nineties decade in season 1990-91, Ossie Ardiles had recently taken over from Jim Smith as boss, however the former Spurs and Argentinean World Cup winner was finding it hard to come to terms with the pressure of rebuilding an ailing club. The following year Newcastle slumped to bottom of the Second Division table for only the fourth time in their history. Ardiles had to do something special to halt a slide that was sending Newcastle United into Division Three in what was their official Centenary Year. At the same time, actions off the football field were creating headlines with Sir John Hall's Magpie Group making a sustained bid to control the club.

Sir John Hall, the Tyneside entrepreneur and property developer, eventually gained part control of the Magpies which resulted in a boardroom restructuring in November 1991. However, at the very first meeting of the new management, United fans witnessed a shock coup. It was a move that came about because of the horrendous economic plight of the club. Sir John noted, "We are haemorrhaging money at the rate of between £600,000 and £700,000 a year in interest charges. The financial position is such that we have reached a point where I couldn't sit on the sidelines any longer". United's worsening position needed drastic action, and very quickly.

Sir John Hall, who rescued an ailing club and transformed The Magpies.

Newcastle needed Sir John's financial muscle and business acumen. He took on the biggest challenge of his life, to transform United into the one of football's super-clubs with his enterprise and drive. In the coming months the Cameron Hall empire would overhaul the club from top to bottom. He was one step away from a complete take-over and rebirth of the Magpies. For the next few months a power struggle developed as the old regime battled to counter Sir John's dynamism. Eventually the Magpie Group succeeded, and Newcastle United never looked back.

In the dressing-room Ardiles had little to offer in attempting to reverse his side's flagging fortunes. The board recognised they had to make a change and rapidly to have any chance of saving the club from relegation. Following a low point in an away fixture against Oxford during February 1992, a game in which the black'n'whites lost 5-2, Ardiles was sacked and immediately replaced by Kevin Keegan – out of football since leaving the Magpies back in 1984.

But Newcastle's board, and Chief Executive Freddie Fletcher in particular, were always convinced that only one man could lead Newcastle out of the relegation mire. Keegan had the Midas touch, he was an inspiration and considered almost super-human to the legions of United supporters who longed for someone to lead and motivate them.

When Kevin Keegan took over at St James Park it was a sensational appointment which captured the whole nation's imagination. Installed as a consultant-manager until the end of the season, he had one job — to save the club from relegation. Failure would almost certainly result in the club going under. That was unthinkable, but a real possibility.

Keegan's charisma was never in doubt. He had to lift an indifferent team out of the relegation zone. And that was always going to be a tough task. But he received the backing of the board and the fans. Supporters flocked back to St James Park, just as they had done in 1982 when Keegan first arrived. Gallowgate – and the whole of Tyneside – buzzed with football fever. Attendances had dwindled to an average of 17,267 but with Keegan's arrival the gate jumped dramatically to almost 30,000.

The former England skipper inspired his players too and by the time the do or die confrontation took place at Filbert Street, Leicester at the end of the season, United had been on a roller-coaster of emotions as they fought against the drop. Keegan used all his motivating skills to gee up his team for the final contest against promotion chasing Leicester. He noted, "We need a result, but we'll get it, survive and take-off". And Newcastle did exactly what the manager predicted.

In a white-hot atmosphere Gavin Peacock gave United a first-half lead, but Leicester rallied and grabbed a late equaliser to the agony of the massed United support. However Peacock was always a menace and Newcastle immediately hit-back in the dying minutes as United's star-man forced defender Steve Walsh into an injury time own-goal to give the Magpies a deserved 2-1 victory. Three points which guaranteed Second Division football and with it, the Magpies' future. United's triumph in adversity was the turning point in Newcastle's fortunes.

Following United's amazing escape from the brink, Sir John Hall quickly moved to consolidate his position in control of affairs at St James Park. Rapidly the Chairman made decisive moves behind the scenes to force a total take-over. Backed by his son Douglas and Tyneside businessman Freddie Shepherd, as well as the considerable drive of Freddie Fletcher, the new managerial team persuaded Kevin Keegan to take a full-time appointment as boss during the summer of 1992.

Immediately the new duo of Hall and Keegan swung into action. The Chairman began planning a vast transformation of St James Park and overhaul of the club's finances. Keegan began to build for the coming 1992-93 season. Cash was released, despite the growing debts – now effectively underwritten by the Cameron-Hall multi-million pound empire. Together they proved a dynamic pairing.

Keegan, supported ably by his assistant, former United and Liverpool star Terry McDermott, made three key signings in the summer months bringing versatile defender Barry Venison from Liverpool, John

Kevin Keegan built a side that very nearly lifted the Premiership title.

Beresford north from Portsmouth and luring Sunderland's skipper Paul Bracewell from Wear to Tyne. He was to splash out another £700,000 early into the season on Charlton Athletic's highly rated striker and midfield player Robert Lee. And the ambition was there for all to see when a huge £3m bid – alas an unsuccessful one – was made to land Southampton's goalpoacher Alan Shearer.

Newcastle opened the new season in stunning fashion. They roared to a victorious start and simply could not stop winning! United registered ten wins out of ten games played, a maximum of 30 points, and galloped clear of the First Division field. The country took notice as the Tynesiders began to capture the nation's imagination. Displaying a brand of football full of attacking ideas, tremendous workrate, great spirit, as well as a solid back four, Newcastle reached 11 victories in succession with a splendid performance against Sunderland at Roker Park.

That notable success took United in sight of the record books, but then unfashionable Grimsby Town arrived at Gallowgate and spoiled the party, winning with a last minute goal. Yet Newcastle's run had been quite sensational, especially when compared to the previous season's efforts. It was the springboard that Keegan needed. United were clear at the top of the table. A buzz of anticipation covered Tyneside. Both players and supporters were on the crest of a wave. The sleeping giant had awoken.

Before the final run-in to the season, Keegan splashed out in the transfer market. Scott Sellars came from Leeds United and during March the manager broke the club's record transfer by paying £1.75m for Bristol City's exciting young striker Andy Cole. Although the big fee United paid was classed by many as a gamble for a player with limited experience, Keegan's judgement was proved ever so right. Cole rapidly developed into a natural goalscorer with devastating pace and expert placement of his shot. Within a few short months he was the new Number 9 hero to the Toon Army.

Newcastle clinched promotion into the Premier League with a fixture at Grimsby Town during May. A Geordie invasion engulfed Cleethorpes and Blundell Park and they witnessed a 2-0 scoreline and with it joyous scenes on the final whistle. Partying lasted all week with the final home fixture of the season against Leicester City proving a fitting finale to a marvellous season.

Newcastle were crowned Football League Champions with all the pomp and celebration of a club that had yearned for success for so long. And then the black'n'whites turned on a performance that astounded everyone, including millions on television. At half-time they ran off to rapturous acclaim 6-0 ahead! They tore Leicester apart – a good side already in the play-offs — with brilliant team play. With Newcastle going onto win 7-1, both David Kelly and Andy Cole registered hat-tricks.

Activity was hectic at St James Park during the summer months of 1993 as Newcastle United made sure they were ready on and off the field for their first taste of the FA Carling Premiership. Ground redevelopment was well underway and manager Keegan had money to spend. Media speculation was rife that several players were heading north to Tyneside.

The signing to catch the public's imagination was the £1.5m homecoming of Peter Beardsley who returned to Tyneside from Everton. At over 30 years of age some doubted the wisdom of paying so much for a player at the end of his career, but Keegan knew his man. Beardsley was to be the key player in a United side that took the Premiership by storm.

Yet the Magpies had to cope without their little playmaker for the opening weeks after he sustained a broken jaw, and took a while to come to terms with the higher standard of football. United though, gradually found their feet and displayed a brand of football that gave Keegan's men the tag of The Entertainers. An emphatic 3-0 success over Liverpool was the benchmark in United's progress. For long the men from Liverpool had dominated in Tyne-Mersey clashes. Now it was Newcastle's turn. The Anfield side were outplayed and outclassed by a slick moving Magpie machine with Andy Cole – fast becoming a noted centre-forward – grabbing a first-half hat-trick. United also took three points from the return meeting at Anfield to emphasise their newly found status.

Midway through the season a significant moment took place when Kevin Keegan signed a ten year contract. Keegan had shown in a short time that he was capable of managing a top side – few on Tyneside ever doubted that, but many away from the region had to be convinced. He had transformed the Magpies from an outfit facing the Third Division trapdoor to one capable of challenging for the Premier League title, importantly in a style that impressed everyone.

Newcastle's manager soon splashed out in the transfer market now that cash was rolling into the Gallowgate bank account from every angle. Keegan spent over £2m on Norwich City's exciting winger Ruel Fox and then £2.7m on QPR centre-half Darren Peacock. Both were record signings for the Magpies.

Newcastle ended the 1993-94 season on a high. During March they played five games and won five games with a total of 17 goals scored. Included was a magnificent seven against poor Swindon Town on Tyneside. Newcastle targeted a European place and thrashed Aston Villa by five goals, on the day that Andy Cole grabbed his 40th goal of the season to create a new scoring record for the club. Newcastle finished in a creditable 3rd place behind Champions Manchester United and Blackburn Rovers. They ended the season as the Premiership's record goalscorers with 82 goals. They were back in the big-time.

At the start of the 1994-95 season many in the game tipped United for a trophy that Kevin Keegan was desperate to bring to Tyneside. Sir John Hall was looking further ahead, he noted, "My ambition is to see this club, within the next five years, established as one of the top three in the United Kingdom and, over the next ten years, amongst the top ten in Europe".

New faces arrived on Tyneside as Keegan continued his policy of being a buying manager. World Cup stars from USA 94, Belgium's Philippe Albert and Switzerland's Marc Hottiger were added to the squad and later Paul Kitson came from Derby County. As the campaign started the Magpies' flowing football was on song. Passing was quick, accurate and the one-touch interplay was a pleasure to watch. And when they got into the box defenders couldn't handle the Cole led attack.

In Europe United thrashed Royal Antwerp 11-2 on aggregate in the UEFA Cup. Newcastle recorded a club record of nine wins in a row and not surprisingly were top of the Premiership and opening up a points gap. But the promising start was not sustained. Following an exit in the UEFA Cup to Athletic Bilbao the side appeared to have been affected by that Euro exit and consistency was difficult to maintain. They were also ravaged by injury for the rest of the season and looked second best to Manchester United and Blackburn Rovers in the title race. Both clubs were to pass the black'n'whites as Newcastle slipped down the table and missed a European place.

And the disappointing season also saw Keegan stun the football world by selling the new King of Tyneside, Andy Cole to rivals Manchester United for a record £7m – then an unheard of sum in

England. Cole had not asked for a move, but Keegan had decided to cash in on the goalscoring gem he had turned from an unknown into a hero. United's manager was intent on a change in strategy. He now had over £10m to bolster his squad and find a replacement for Cole.

The manager could also rely on extra funds from his board who backed Keegan to the limit. The club's tremendous economic recovery continued unabated. Before Sir John Hall took the Magpies under his control, turnover was a modest £4m in 1990 and less than £9m in the financial year ending 1993. By the time the club had concluded their first season in the Premier League it had shot up to £17m, projected to reach over £40m by the end of the decade. St James Park was at capacity for every game. They were now second only to Manchester United in financial muscle.

United's boss was determined to make sure that he had a squad to sustain a long Premiership season and make a serious bid for silverware. In the close season of 1995 that saw millions of pounds exchange hands for top players from home and abroad, Newcastle United led the way and created football fever on Tyneside. Wimbledon's Warren Barton was purchased for £4m, then Keegan landed his replacement for Andy Cole, paying £6m for Les Ferdinand from QPR. Soon after he brought the talented Paris St Germain forward David Ginola to England, a signing that captivated the Toon Army – and then spent more on goalkeeper Shaka Hislop. Keegan had assembled a formidable squad, one that was to take Manchester United all the way in the title race.

For much of the 1995-96 season Newcastle United had everything absolutely right. They roared to the top of the table and had a comfortable points advantage over their rivals from Old Trafford. Their football was scintillating. In attack, Les Ferdinand was outstanding, served on each wing by Ginola and Keith Gillespie who arrived at Gallowgate as part of the Cole deal. Peter Beardsley and Rob Lee were prompting from midfield and grabbing goals too. Newcastle played like and looked like stylish Champions. And soon to be added to the squad were England's David Batty who arrived from Blackburn, and the Colombian international Tino Asprilla, who cost £7.5m from Italian club Parma. It seemed that Keegan could not be stopped in lifting the club's first Title trophy since 1927.

Over the Christmas period United held a lead of ten points over Manchester United, but a defeat by the Reds at Old Trafford was a crucial blow which United never really recovered from. And the pressure from all quarters mounted on the players and manager – not to mention the supporters. The crucial run-in to the title started with a momentous clash with Manchester United at St James Park. It was a game that the black'n'whites needed to win to keep the Reds at bay. And they played to form as they dominated a match but could not score, then watched in agony as Eric Cantona stole the points to put the Reds back in the hunt for the Championship trophy.

United lost to Arsenal, then took part in a thrilling but heart-breaking encounter with Liverpool at Anfield. Newcastle lost 4-3 with a last minute goal from Stan Collymore. Newcastle kept winning their home games, but couldn't hold onto leads when away from Tyneside. United then faced three crucial away games in 6 days as the season reached its peak, a week which would decide the destination of the Premier League trophy.

Newcastle travelled to face Blackburn Rovers and dominated the match. David Batty gave United a 1-0 advantage with only 15 minutes left of the contest. United had one hand on the title trophy. But Newcastle's Achilles heel – their inability to defend stoutly when in front – caused their downfall. In the dying seconds Blackburn's substitute Graham Fenton — ironically a Geordie – netted twice to grab the points from the Tynesider's grasp.

United won at Leeds thanks to a Keith Gillespie goal, then faced Nottingham Forest at the City Ground. Again the Magpies had one hand on the silverware when Peter Beardsley's glorious goal hit the back of the net and then missed several chances to claim the points. To the frustration of their fans, once more they let the game slip when Ian Woan crashed home a characteristic long range shot for the equaliser.

The Championship was now in Manchester United's hands and they didn't let it slip. They won the title with Newcastle a demoralised runner-up after leading the pack for most of the season. Peter Beardsley was to record in his biography, "We had ourselves to blame", while Kevin Keegan noted in the club's magazine, "We have played some wonderful football and I'm well aware that most of the neutral fans in this country feel that we've entertained them better than any other club. But that's not a consolation – I wanted Newcastle United to be champions and we're not the champions".

The result of that title race was to effect United in the following season, although to start with Keegan was doubly determined to win that elusive but most important trophy in the country. The football world was shocked as Newcastle United paid a world record fee of £15m to bring Alan Shearer back to his native Tyneside during the summer, a deal that showed the rest of the game that the club were indeed a big player – and intent in claiming success on the field.

Shearer's purchase was a coup. Hailed the best centre-forward in Europe at the time, his Geordie background gave him massive fan support and the pairing of Ferdinand and Shearer up front was to prove a devastating combination. Newcastle though, started with something of a hangover from the previous season's title race. They lost embarrassingly to Manchester United in the FA Charity Shield and took a while to develop tactics to suit the Shearer-Ferdinand double strike-force. But after a victory at Roker Park, Sunderland, the team clicked and goals flowed, culminating in a wonderful 5-0 revenge victory over Manchester United at St James Park. Newcastle were back on top of the table again and favourites to lift the Championship.

But fate was not on Newcastle's side. Injuries disrupted plans with crucially both Shearer and Ferdinand out for spells. United slipped from top spot. And behind the scenes the club was going through a major flotation to transform the club into a plc – a move that was to raise massive funds, but also rock the foundations as Kevin Keegan became a high profile casualty.

The pressure that had mounted on the manager was immense. Last season's championship failure had taken its toll on Keegan – even to the point of resignation. And the floatation required a commitment from Newcastle's boss that he would be around as United developed from a private company to one publicly owned. That was not forthcoming and relationships between manager and certain sections of the board deteriorated. Events came to a head over the New Year holiday period when after almost five years in charge Kevin Keegan left Newcastle with bitterness. During January the football world was stunned as the Magpies had to find a new man to lead their challenge. Sir John Hall said in Black and White magazine, "The job he did for us was just phenomenal. He has lifted our stature to such an extent that we are now recognised as one of the top clubs in Europe".

Newcastle's directors did not take long to appoint a new manager. Within days Kenny Dalglish was installed at St James Park – one of the few men who could step into Keegan's shoes. With a track record as a player and manager second to none, he appeared the ideal choice. But there was to be a stark contrast between the two as Dalglish began to dismantle Keegan's bright, entertaining line-up, full of goals and big names and develop his own less flamboyant outfit which found goals hard to come by, resulting in the entertainment value dropping alarmingly.

But to start with most United supporters were content with the appointment and Dalglish took time to assess the squad he had inherited. Most judges considered all the new manager had to do was to add two or three players to Keegan's squad – especially at the back to strengthen the defence. For the remaining programme of the 1996-97 season, Dalglish guided United on the right tracks for a European place again. Without hitting the headlines, the Magpies even found themselves with an outside chance of the title as the last month of the season unfolded. Newcastle took the points at Arsenal and had to win at West Ham to have any chance of catching Manchester United in the title race. But United could only draw and the Reds once again lifted the trophy. Newcastle though, following a 5-0 victory over Nottingham Forest, clinched their second successive Runners-up spot and with it a place in the new and highly lucrative European Champions League.

Season 1997-98 was to be another campaign of highs and lows. Dalglish began wheeling and dealing in the transfer market. One of the first players to go was the popular and matchwinning genius of David Ginola who joined Tottenham. Quickly to follow was Les Ferdinand, also sold to Spurs, ironically during the same weekend that Alan Shearer fractured his fibula and badly ruptured ligaments. Newcastle supporters were not happy. After boasting the best pair of strikers in the Premiership, backed by the best provider, Newcastle had lost them all. Dalglish brought in a line of new faces, including veterans Ian Rush, John Barnes and Stuart Pearce. None though were in the same top quality mould as Keegan's signings.

The black'n'whites entered the Champions League with a patched up line-up and after qualifying with a two legged victory against Croatia Zagreb, Newcastle were drawn in the Group stage alongwith Dynamo Kiev, PSV and the mighty Barcelona. It was a quite a test. But Newcastle did have one player in Tino Asprilla who kept his best football for European occasions. The temperamental Colombian had not been a great success in Premiership action, but did continually find the net when in continental mode.

United opened their Champions League campaign with an epic against Barcelona at Gallowgate. It was a game beamed around the world and Newcastle showed impressive style as they stormed into a 3-0 lead with a brilliant Asprilla hat-trick. Although the Spanish giants pulled two goals back late into the game, Newcastle's performance was hailed as one of their best ever. For an hour they outclassed Barcelona and around 200 million enthusiasts watched around the world on television.

After that opening Newcastle struggled in their remaining games, mainly due to injury problems, losing Asprilla on top of their loss of both Ferdinand and Shearer. They drew in Kiev but lost both games against the Dutch, and lost 1-0 on a rain soaked evening in Barcelona. Failing to qualify for the next stage United signed off with a 2-0 home victory over Dynamo Kiev, the group's top team.

In domestic football Dalglish's side also struggled to maintain a Premiership challenge. During the second half of the season Newcastle were heading down the table rather than up and were threatened with relegation at one low point. However, in the FA Cup, United went all the way to Wembley with the return of Alan Shearer from injury giving the side a major boost. After defeating Everton and going through an uncomfortable tie – both on and off the pitch – against non-leaguers Stevenage Borough, United reached the Sixth Round with a victory over Tranmere Rovers. The magic of the FA Cup had now captivated Tyneside and a comfortable win over Barnsley took United into the semi-final with Sheffield United at Old Trafford.

Tino Asprilla shakes hands with the referee at the final whistle of the Champions League clash with Barcelona.

A single goal from Alan Shearer was enough to give the Toon Army a Wembley final, but United had never been too convincing and many feared for the outcome in the meeting with eventual Double winners Arsenal at the Twin Towers. And on the day the Gunners were far too clever for a subdued and negative United side, Newcastle losing 2-0. The display was as disappointing as the Championship race in 1995, and Kenny Dalglish quickly lost many of his newly found Geordie allies on that afternoon.

During the summer of 1997 United's boss went on a spending spree in a bid to revitalise his side. Internationals like Germany's Didi Hamman, Peru's Nol Solano and French World Cup winner Stephane Guivarc'h all arrived, while Kevin Keegan's side had all been totally dismantled. Expectation on Tyneside though was as high as ever. Following the frustration of the FA Cup final display with Arsenal and concluding the season in a lowly Premiership placing, Dalglish appeared determined to regain the Magpies' status as an exciting Premier League force.

But not for the first time – or no doubt the last – Newcastle United hit the headlines just as the season began. Kenny Dalglish departed to the delight of many Newcastle supporters, and another high profile manager took control, this time former Chelsea boss and one of the world's greatest players, Dutch ace Ruud Gullit. The new appointment was heralded with much elation and as a new starting point in regaining the club's position as the country's most favourite side, gained with Kevin Keegan's Entertainers, but lost under the guidance of Dalglish.

Ruud Gullit was quick to point out that he would need time and money to rebuild the St James Park staff. He quite rightly took a period to assess the playing squad he had inherited, one that had lost a flamboyant and stylish content so favoured on Tyneside. He was not slow to note that he needed to make changes. Out went Guivarc'h, as did David Batty, John Barnes and local favourite Steve Watson, sold to raise funds. More would have been sold, but Gullit was restricted with limited interest in Dalglish's players. In came young French full-back Didier Domi from Paris St Germain for over £3m and Scottish international striker Duncan Ferguson arrived in a big £8m deal from Everton. Unluckily Ferguson was soon sidelined with a bad injury that kept him out of action for most of the campaign. Later in the season Croatia Zagreb's talented forward Silvio Maric joined Gullit's new look staff.

In between the transfer activity, United's season was an inconsistent one. The Premiership programme was disjointed, the Magpies hovering in mid-table or occasionally slipping dangerously close to the relegation dogfight. Only once did they put a sustained run together, that shortly after Gullit's arrival when they reached 5th place in the table following three league victories in a row.

Newcastle fell in the Football League Cup to Blackburn Rovers after a 1-1 draw and a penalty shoot-out that favoured the Ewood club. In the UEFA Cup Winners Cup, again the black'n'whites did not venture far. Drawn against experienced European campaigners Partizan Belgrade, United took a 2-1 lead to Yugoslavia, but went out of the competition on the away goals after losing by a single goal in the Slav capital. It had been a tense and fiery atmosphere to cope with, as only a few months later NATO and Britain were at war with Yugoslavia over Kosovo.

It was left to the FA Cup to provide Newcastle's fervent Toon Army with something to shout about. And just like last season the black'n'whites dished up a rousing run to Wembley – again though without being totally convincing on the field. Newcastle had fortune on their side too, as the luck of the draw saw the Magpies playing all their opening four rounds of the competition at Gallowgate.

Former Newcastle boss Ruud Gullit.

Struggling Crystal Palace arrived first, but fell, then Bradford City suffered the same fate. Blackburn Rovers provided tougher opposition. They aimed to give Newcastle a double cup knock-out and held United to a 0-0 draw and earned a replay at Ewood Park. However, Newcastle put together a battling display in Lancashire and on loan striker Louis Saha took a brilliant Hamann long cross field ball to fire into the net and send United a step closer to Wembley.

In the quarter-final Everton travelled to Tyneside attempting to stop United's successive Wembley bid. For a period they foiled the Magpies, but a late rally saw Newcastle victorious by 4-1 with popular Georgian Temuri Ketsbaia putting on a five star show. United were back at Old Trafford for the semi-final, scene of last year's jubilation after defeating Sheffield United. This time George Graham's Tottenham Hotspur stood between the Tynesiders and another cup final. It was a side that included former Toon heroes Les Ferdinand and David Ginola, who had displayed top form in the season to earn both Footballer of the Year awards to the frustration of Newcastle's fans.

For ninety minutes a tense affair took place without many clear-cut openings, but in extra-time and with Duncan Ferguson on as sub even though he was not fully fit, Newcastle took control. Alan Shearer converted a penalty then hit a screamer into the top corner of the net to make sure it was going to be a Geordie fanfare at Wembley again.

The Wembley occasion in 1999 had a deja vu feeling about it. Up against Manchester United this time, Newcastle were clearly second best, and although defeated by the eventual treble winners, the Magpies did perform better than against the Gunners in 1998. Crucial moments of the match sealed United's fate; a bad defensive mistake gave away a second killer goal, and two misses, one by Ketsbaia – who hit a post – and by Maric, that would have put the black'n'whites back in the match.

Considering the changes made in the 1998-99 season though, the season ended with reasonable satisfaction. Reaching Wembley and Europe was a huge bonus. Ruud Gullit's rebuilding process was well under way with more new signings scheduled to be on Tyneside for the start of the Millennium season. But to Newcastle United supporters, four Runners-up positions in four successive seasons – two in the Premier League and two in the FA Cup – was hard to take. Newcastle's manager though had the confidence of the vast majority of Magpies supporters. And with new international players like Spain's Marcelino, Alain Goma of France as well as the young talent of Kieron Dyer, already in the England full squad, the days of becoming The Entertainers once again and lifting their first modern trophy may just be around the corner.

However, in true Newcastle united tradition of hitting the headlines, manager Hullit sensationally resigned after only three weeks of the new season.

The task of taking forward the Magpies, now one of the biggest clubs in Europe, into the Millennium was to be left to another personality in the form of England manager, and local hero, Bobby Robson...

Newcastle's £8 million striker, Scottish internationalist Duncan Ferguson.

England and Magpie skipper Alan Shearer.

UNITED'S MODERN RECORD

Season	League Position		FAC	FLC	Euro
1990-91	Division Two	11th	R4	R2	
1991-92	Division Two	20th	R3	R3	
1992-93	Division One	1st	R5	R3	
1993-94	Premier League	3rd	R4	R3	
1994-95	Premier League	6th	R6	R4	UEFA Cup R2
1995-96	Premier League	2nd	R3	R5	
1996-97	Premier League	2nd	R4	R4	UEFA Cup R4
1997-98	Premier League	13th	Final	R5	Champ Lg Group
1998-99	Premier League	13th	Final	R4	ECWC R1

Les Ferdinand, such a popular player with The Toon Army.

HUMBLE ORIGINS

Football in its modern form arouses passions on Tyneside like no other sport or pastime. Yet the North East region was one of the country's late developers and not until around 1890 did Tyneside see rapid progress made, several years after other parts of the country had seen football flourish. Even then support was a trickle compared to the 65,000 crowds that were to roar encouragement to Newcastle United in their heyday and the 51,000 that will watch the Magpies at the new St James Park in the Millennium.

The first recorded game of football on Tyneside took place on 3rd March 1877 at the Elswick Rugby Club when a few keen enthusiasts formed two scratch teams – eight against nine – the nine winning 2-0. Shortly afterwards Newcastle's first club was born, Tyne Association being formed in 1877. Another side, Newcastle Rangers started life in 1878 and first played on the Drill Field at Gateshead because they could not find a pitch north of the river. They eventually moved across the Tyne taking over an enclosed ground close to Leazes Terrace in September 1880. The pitch was immediately referred to as St James Park. The foundation had been laid in Newcastle United's development.

The year of 1882 was an important 12 months in the history of the club as two new sides arrived on the scene which eventually were to lead to the present-day Magpies. Newcastle United's origins are to be found with two minor football clubs on the east of the city, Stanley and Rosewood. Stanley had originated from a cricket eleven, formed in November 1881 – the rudimentary start of Newcastle United, although some official records note that the club were playing an unorganised game a year earlier.

As Stanley progressed with their pioneering game, they were often confused with other clubs of the same name in County Durham, so they decided to change their title in October 1882 to Newcastle East End. Rosewood had been formed a couple of months earlier and soon joined forces with East End to form a stronger outfit, their side being integrated as East End's reserve eleven.

In the summer of 1884 East End moved the short distance from Stanley Street in Byker to a new pitch close by, then again two years later to Chillingham Road, near to the sprawling railway network on the Byker and Heaton border.

On the other side of the city at the same time as East End were taking shape, another club was born which had much to do with the evolution of Newcastle United. Again their origins lay with the game of cricket. At West End Cricket Club more enthusiasts of the new association code decided also to switch to football. In August 1882 West End Football Club was set-up, almost a year after Stanley had first kicked off. West End played their football on a cricket field on the Town Moor, but moved in the summer of 1885 to a pitch off the Great North Road. They moved once more a year later in May 1886 and took over the lease of St James Park.

With East End and West End on the football map the first stage in the development of Newcastle United was complete. The men who made the club on their respective sides of the city were a mixed bunch; professionals, businessmen, shopkeepers and tradesmen. Many both administered and played the game as it took root. East End were represented by the likes of William Findlay and Alex White, while West End had William Nesham and John Black. Tom Watson was also at West End, but he was to switch camps and be an influential figure at East End.

An early group of Newcastle East End, pictured at their Chillingham Road ground.

West End's first game was on 7th October, 1882, against Rosewood, a 2-0 defeat just before the Byker side were to amalgamate with the newly titled East End. A mile across the city, East End kicked off on the same day against Hamsterley Rangers at Byker and faired better, winning 1-0. The East Enders though, unlike their rivals, had at least a feel for the new game having played several matches under the banner of Stanley.

Football, of course, was very different in those pioneering days. There were no club sponsors or business suites, no private-boxes or restaurants. No sophisticated tactical plans and no highly paid mega-stars. Players were initially amateurs, although they did receive illegal payments, then became part-timers employed in the many local industries on Tyneside. The dribbling game was the norm at first. When a player got the ball he simply ran with it until he scored or was dispossessed. Tactics and combination play evolved slowly. Pitch markings were different too, with a goal box of two semi-circular areas for many years. Goal nets had not been invented and in many places cloth tapes acted as a cross-bar, while free-kicks and penalties were just being thought about.

By 1884 both East End and West End had emerged as Tyneside's strongest sides, overtaking the original pioneers Tyne and Rangers. Both clubs also started to take part in the competition in which Newcastle United was to carve a special niche; the FA Cup. Formed as far back as 1871, West End was the first of the two rivals to appear in the tournament. In 1886 they played Sunderland and won the match after a controversial contest only to loose to Gainsborough Trinity in the next round. Twelve months later East End made their FA Cup debut. They played South Bank on Tees-side, but lost 3-2 after extra-time.

Newcastle West End started to show up as the stronger of the two rivals at first. They made headlines during the summer months of 1888 by attracting Scottish internationalist Bob Kelso to St James Park. He was the biggest personality by far to appear regularly for a Tyneside club, having made a name for himself as a right-half with Renton, then a prominent force north of the border.

East End knew they had to make changes to keep up with the ambitious West Enders. In the same close season they lured Tom Watson from St James Park and underwent drastic surgery in both players and officials, an overhaul that was to eventually revive their fortunes.

In April 1888 the Football League was set up in Manchester when twelve clubs agreed to try a new venture that would ensure the game of football would spread rapidly. Newcastle clubs were not part of it, although Wearside teams, Sunderland and Sunderland Albion, were soon to apply for membership. Tyneside's clubs had no such thoughts yet and were content to help form a local Northern League which consisted of ten founder clubs, a mix of professionals and amateurs. For season 1889-90 league football of sorts arrived on Tyneside. West End did well, finishing runners-up to Darlington St Augustine. East End were fourth in the inaugural table.

As the Nineties decade opened football was progressing quickly. Goal nets arrived and a team game – albeit a primitive one – replaced the solo free-for-all. At this time East End took a bold and huge leap forward in a bid to oust their West End rivals from prominence. They decided in 1890 to become a Limited Company with an issue of 2,000 shares at 10 shillings each – the very same shares at the centre of the battle for control of Newcastle United nearly a century later. Not wanting to be left behind West End quickly followed suit. The venture was not to prove an instant recipe for success, but within 18 months it was the East Enders, and not West End, that developed into Tyneside's top club.

The battle for prominence between the two camps continued. East End by now were heading up the

East End's great rivals, Newcastle West End.

table and coming to grips with the blossoming game. West End, however were heading the other way, in rapid decline. The Chillingham Road club possessed more talented players, displayed better football, could attract larger gates, although still pitifully small, and had a much more enterprising management.

One underlying fact remained clear. The city was not big enough for two football clubs. There was only support to ensure the development of the association game for one set-up. If football was to progress further, one club had to go and by the end of the 1891-92 season Newcastle West End's position, both on the field and at the bank, had become perilous. Their Northern League results were dreadful and they were out of funds.

At the end of April 1892 the St James Park club was on the brink of insolvency and extinction. West End offered their lease of St James Park to East End alongwith taking over what remained of the club's assets, including their players. Within a week a deal had been agreed and in May 1892 East End formally agreed to move home to the more advantageous St James Park base near the city centre. Tyneside now only had one senior club and they developed rapidly thereafter.

Before the start of the new 1892-93 season, East End's new set-up attempted to gain entry into the Football League, at a time when the competition had only a single division. At the annual meeting held in Sunderland, the East Enders were refused entry to the First Division after polling a mere one vote. However, the Tynesiders were admitted to a newly formed Second Division as one of the largely unknown and untried beginners. The club's officials though, did not relish the thought of Second Division opposition, as few clubs possessed the drawing power for which East End craved. They wanted the likes of Preston North End, Everton, Sunderland and Aston Villa at St James Park and with them much increased gates and of course revenue. They saw Second Division clubs like Bootle and Crewe as being no better than the past season's Northern League opposition. So East End declined the invitation and waited patiently for the chance to go national for another day.

East End's – and in essence – Newcastle United's first game at St James Park took place on 3rd September 1892 against Glasgow Celtic, a prestigious friendly won 1-0 by the visitors before a healthy 6,000 crowd. But crowds of that size were rare. Support was poor and in a bid to attract more spectators from Victorian Tyneside it was decided that radical changes had to be implemented. At a meeting during December in the Bath Lane Hall – a goal kick from St James Park – East End's directors presided over a large gathering of football enthusiasts. An open discussion on the future of football on Tyneside took place and one of the points agreed was the need to dispose of the old title of Newcastle East End in a bid to attract a wider support from the city as a whole. Several names were suggested, but voting was almost unanimous for Newcastle United. So on Friday 9th December 1892, East End became Newcastle United, although the legal title of the club was not altered for several years to come.

One facet of East End's existence remained though. The club, for the time being at any rate, still retained their colours of red and white stripes. The famous black'n'whites striped shirt was not to arrive until 1894.

The following summer, in 1893, the Tynesiders attempted to gain entry into the First Division of the Football League once more. However, again the game's authorities would not accept United's direct entry into the top division and for a second time, offered United the opportunity of Second Division status. Newcastle were desperate to get involved in the national game as they, rightly so, were convinced it was the only way to increase revenue in the long term. So this time United accepted. Also to be elected were Liverpool and Arsenal – a momentous day for the game. Newcastle United became a member of the Football League and were on their way to over a century of action.

MILESTONES

1881
Newcastle United's pioneer club, Stanley of Byker are formed. They play their first game against the Elswick Leather Works second eleven and win 5-0.

1882
The Club's other founding team, Newcastle West End begin life, while in October, Stanley change their name to Newcastle East End to begin a city rivalry to eventually develop into Newcastle United. East End's first fixture takes place against Hamsterley Rangers, a 1-0 victory.

1886
West End move home to a city centre site called St James Park.

1887
East End take part in the FA Cup for the first time when they compete with South Bank but lose 3-2.

1889
Both East End and West End turn professional as the game of football develops from its amateur roots on Tyneside.

1890
Each club announces that Limited Companies have been formed and make a share issue to the local public. East End float capital of £1,000 in 10-shilling shares. Both sides join the new Northern League competition.

1892
A notable year in the history of the Magpies as Newcastle West End fold due to financial problems and East End agree to take-over the lease of their ground at St James Park. They also incorporate most of the players and directors within their set-up. Only one major club remains on Tyneside. At the end of the year East End agree to change their name to Newcastle United.

1893
During the close season Newcastle United are elected to the Football League alongwith other notable names of the future, Liverpool and Arsenal. They play their first league fixture in September against the Gunners in London and draw 2-2. Tyneside witnesses it's first league encounter, also against Arsenal and Newcastle record a resounding 6-0 victory.

1894
United decide to change their colours from red shirts to the now famous black'n'white striped shirts, although for sometime yet they wore blue shorts.

1895
Newcastle find life in professional football tough, they lose 0-9 to Burton Wanderers in the Second Division and 1-7 against Aston Villa in a FA Cup tie. Both results still stand as record defeats.

1898
The Tynesiders start to make an impact, they gain promotion to the First Division after a series of Test Matches with Stoke, Blackburn Rovers and Burnley. Striker Jock Peddie ends as leading scorer with 18 goals in the season. He is the club's first centre-forward hero.

1899
Newcastle complete their first season in the top flight in a creditable 13th spot. Wolves become United's initial opponents, a 2-4 defeat at Gallowgate before a 20,000 crowd. Newcastle's supporters also witness their first league derby meeting with neighbours Sunderland. United won 3-2 on Wearside.

1901
The year of the notorious Good Friday riot before a planned fixture with Sunderland at St James Park. An estimated crowd of 70,000 congregated at Gallowgate, then a stadium only holding 30,000. The game never kicked-off.

1905
Newcastle are crowned as Football League Champions for the first time and are a whisker away from lifting the coveted Double as they are beaten 2-0 in the FA Cup final by Aston Villa. The Magpies' side is celebrated as an attractive, passing team – one to dominate the rest of the decade. Stars like Colin Veitch, Andy Aitken, Jimmy Howie and Jackie Rutherford become household names.

1906
The black'n'whites return to the FA Cup final at the old Crystal Palace stadium at Sydenham. However, once more they lose at the last hurdle, this time to Everton by a single goal. More noted players earn big reputations; Peter McWilliam, Bill McCracken, Jimmy Lawrence and Bill Appleyard included.

Irish full-back Bill McCracken, a legend of the game.

1907

With a side now packed with famous names, many of them internationals, United lift the Title. Yet, Newcastle create headlines when they are knocked out of the FA Cup in the First Round by non-league Crystal Palace on Tyneside.

1908

United's third FA Cup final visit in four years again ends in disappointment in South London. The Crystal Palace hoodoo strikes once more as the Magpies fall 3-1 to Second Division Wolves. Scottish international playmaker Jimmy Howie scores United's first goal in a cup final.

FA Cup semi-final action against Fulham, en-route to United's 1908 cup final.

1909

Newcastle walk away with their third Championship victory in five years – by a record seven clear points. They also reach the FA Cup semi-final, but more sensation unfolds as Sunderland astonishingly win at St James Park by a 9-1 scoreline. New centre-forward, England leader Albert Shepherd is established as a fearsome striker.

1910

United continue their Edwardian dominance and reach yet another FA Cup final. This time the Magpies lift the trophy for the first time, but not at the jinxed Crystal Palace venue where they drew 1-1 with Barnsley. In a replay at Goodison Park, a ground to United's liking, they won 2-0 and bring the trophy back to Tyneside. Albert Shepherd nets two goals, including the first ever penalty kick in a cup final.

1911

Another cup final visit, Newcastle's fifth in seven years. Another draw takes place at the black'n'whites bogey venue of the Palace, this time 0-0 with Bradford City. At Old Trafford in the replay, City lift silverware by winning 1-0 – a new FA Cup trophy which was made fittingly in Bradford.

1915

The First World War brought a halt to national football. United had completed the era being recognised as one of a trio of clubs at the very top of the sport. Three Title victories and five FA Cup finals was evidence enough.

1923

Newcastle's post war rebuilding takes shape and the Magpies complete the First Division season in 4th place. Stan Seymour, Tom McDonald and centre-forward Neil Harris become United's dangermen.

1924

United win through to the FA Cup final after a remarkable run, which included four games with Derby County. And this time the competition has a new home, The Empire Stadium, Wembley. Newcastle immediately take to the Twin Towers and its inspiring surroundings. In only the second ever final at Wembley, United defeat Aston Villa 2-0. Seymour and Harris grab the all important goals.

1927

Led by record signing and Scottish legend, Hughie Gallacher, Newcastle make a bid for the Championship and win the race for the trophy with Huddersfield Town and local rivals Sunderland. A new record crowd is established when United meet Sunderland – a top of the table clash. 67,211 see the Magpies triumphant by a single goal. Gallacher marks the season by scoring 39 senior goals – a club record.

1930

Following such a great period, the Tynesiders decline dramatically and finish the season in a lowly 19th position. Newcastle's board take action and appoint a team manger for the first time, bringing south Rangers and Scotland international Andy Cunningham who acted initially as the first ever player-boss in the top division.

1931

Cunningham starts to fashion his side and makes a modest improvement, however creates much controversy by agreeing to sell hero figure Hughie Gallacher to Chelsea for a near record fee of £10,000. The little Scot soon returns to Gallowgate with his new club and a record crowd of 68,386 turn up to welcome him back to Tyneside – an attendance record which still stands.

1932

Another sensation packed FA Cup run ends with a Wembley triumph. Along the way Newcastle hit Southport 9-0 to register their largest victory in the tournament. The Magpies face Arsenal in the final and after a controversial 90 minutes in which United score with a disputed goal that may have seen the ball go out of play before a decisive cross, Newcastle won 2-1 with centre-forward Jack Allen netting both goals. The match was recorded in the game's history as The Over The Line Final due to the disputed equaliser.

1934

Despite defeating Everton 7-3 and Liverpool 9-2 in the space of seven days over the Christmas period and having noted players like Sammy Weaver in their ranks, United end up being relegated for the first time in their history. The club begins a period of decay in the Second Division.

1935

Andy Cunningham departs and Newcastle appoint former Stoke boss Tom Mather into the manager's position at Gallowgate.

1938

Newcastle find life in Division Two difficult to cope with and the Magpies almost slip down another division when they are saved on goal average from relegation to Division Three. Out of the turmoil former star winger Stan Seymour is appointed to the Board and he begins to rebuild the club from top to bottom.

Skipper Jimmy Nelson leads United out at Wembley in 1932.

1939

World War Two forces the game into regional football, despite the hostilities Seymour continues to model his new Newcastle United. With Mather departed, Seymour is manager of the club in all but name.

1947

With peace restored and football booming, a rejuvenated Newcastle United is the centre of attraction again, the country's best supported club – despite Second Division status. United are big spenders in the transfer market, paying vast sums for the likes of Len Shackleton, Frank Brennan and Joe Harvey, but also introducing homegrown talent like Jackie Milburn and Ernie Taylor. They reach the FA Cup semi-final and just miss out on promotion. With a star-studded side, Newcastle thrash Newport County 13-0 at St James Park, a club and national record. One of those stars, Len Shackleton netted 6 goals – all on his debut!

Joe Harvey is a proud captain of The Magpies immediately after World War Two.

1948

With George Martin at the helm in the manager's office, United return to Division One after a 13 year absence, supported by an amazing average attendance at home fixtures of 56,299, a record which stood for 20 years. Wor Jackie Milburn leads the scorers list with 20 goals.

1949

Newcastle are back with the elite of the game and challenging for the Championship trophy. After being in second position for most of the second half of the season they slip up at the death and loose the Title to Portsmouth. New signings George Robledo and Bobby Mitchell quickly become terrace favourites.

1951

With Stan Seymour in charge once more, Newcastle begin their Fifties period of FA Cup glory. They reach the final and defeat Blackpool 2-0 thanks to a couple of wonderful strikes from Jackie Milburn.

Jackie Milburn's wonderful long-range effort against Blackpool in 1951.

1952

It is back to Wembley Stadium and a return clash with Arsenal in the FA Cup final. And once more Newcastle take to the special Wembley atmosphere and lift the trophy for the second successive year through a single goal netted by Chilean international George Robledo.

1953

Newcastle enter the floodlit age at St James Park with a game against Glasgow Celtic. A crowd of 41,888 see the new innovation – and a 2-0 United victory.

1955

With another new manager appointed in Duggie Livingstone, a Tyne verses Wear derby FA Cup final was a distinct possiblity, but while United won through to Wembley, Sunderland lost to Manchester City in the semi-final. United take care of the Red's victors and lift the FA Cup for the third time in five years with a 3-1 victory. Goals from Milburn – within the first minute of the game – Mitchell and George Hannah seal the glory.

1956

United gain some revenge for the embarrassing 9-1 Sunderland defeat in 1908, by winning 6-1 at Roker Park and 3-1 at Gallowgate in the space of two days. However, the Wearsiders knock the black'n'whites out of the FA Cup quarter-final when yet another Wembley visit was edging closer.

1958

Former Manchester United winger Charlie Mitten takes control of the side, while Len White fills the role of crowd favourite after the departure of Jackie Milburn. Off the pitch, a modern floodlighting system was installed at St James Park comprising four huge pylons, which dominated the city landscape for the next 30 years. The prestigious Football League v Scottish League international fixture marks the event.

1961

Charlie Mitten brings plenty of invention and modern techniques to Gallowgate, but also guides Newcastle into the Second Division after conceding 109 goals. Player power erupts as a dispute with George Eastham heads for the High Court.

1964

With Mitten sacked, Newcastle are now under the control of former skipper Joe Harvey. He steadies the camp and rebuilds for the quickly developing modern era of football. A recovery takes place, but Newcastle hit the headlines by being eliminated from the FA Cup by giantkillers and non-league outfit Bedford Town to add more spice to United's history.

1965

Joe Harvey develops a solid and uncompromising side that lifts the Second Division Championship trophy. A near 60,000 crowd watches United defeat Bolton Wanderers 2-0 to clinch their elevation back into the First Division. Goals from Jim Iley and Willie Penman send Tyneside into celebration.

1968

United qualify for European competition for the first time despite completing the 1967-68 season in only 10th place. Record £80,000 signing Wyn Davies proves a popular choice at centre-forward.

1969

Remarkably, at their first attempt, the Magpies lift the Inter Cities Fairs Cup following a pulsating run to a final meeting with Hungarians Ujpesti Dosza. United win the trophy 6-2 on aggregate and shock the European football scene. Skipper Bobby Moncur hits a hat-trick over the two legged tie, while Bryan Robson develops into a noted goalscorer.

1970

More classic European action as Newcastle reach the quarter-finals of the Fairs Cup before losing narrowly to RSC Anderlecht.

1971

The black 'n'whites continue to entertain, yet be inconsistent. They qualify for European action once more, in the Fairs Cup, and the great Internationale of Milan arrive on Tyneside – and are beaten 2-0 – after an outstanding, but fiery match. Davies and Moncur score the goals.

1972

Newcastle spend a vast sum and a club record fee of £180,000 for Malcolm Macdonald, but still are dumped out of the FA Cup by non-league Hereford United. More stylish players take to the field in Terry Hibbitt, Tony Green and Jimmy Smith.

1974

With a flamboyant, but inconsistent side, United return to Wembley in the FA Cup. Yet the black'n'whites do not perform on the day and allow Liverpool to dominate the match and win 3-0. Malcolm Macdonald strikes 25 goals in the season and continues to be a devastating force in attack.

1976

Joe Harvey steps aside and Gordon Lee takes the managerial reigns. He guides Newcastle to another Wembley appearance, this time in the Football League Cup competition. Newcastle perform better despite the squad having suffered with a flu bug, but loose 2-1 to Manchester City. Alan Gowling nets for the black'n'whites, however, Lee then sells goal hero Macdonald to Arsenal.

Celebration for Glenn Keeley, Geoff Nutty and Alan Gowling after reaching Wembley in 1976.

1977

Manager Gordon Lee resigns under controversy and his assistant Richard Dinnis takes control. United complete the season in 5th place – their highest position since 1951 — and win a place in the UEFA Cup.

1978
After internal turmoil over the managership of Richard Dinnis, which almost resulted in a players' strike, and the appointment of Bill McGarry as boss, United find themselves back in the Second Division.

1981
As in the Thirties, the black'n'whites do not come to grips with Second Division football quickly. McGarry moves on to be replaced by Arthur Cox, but the Magpies continue to struggle to make an impact on the promotion race.

1983
Former England skipper Kevin Keegan joins United in a sensational move, from Southampton, which captivates the whole of Tyneside. Keegan's presence starts an amazing revival and with it an equally amazing bond develops between supporters and superstar.

1984
Keegan leads Newcastle to promotion after a season of quality football featuring up and coming youngsters Peter Beardsley and Chris Waddle. However, United's celebrations are halted as manager Arthur Cox resigns and England World Cup winner Jack Charlton is appointed to the Geordie hot-seat.

1985
Before the start of the new season Charlton is stung by supporters criticism over his style of play as well as lack of transfer activity and steps down as manager. United turn to former goalkeeper and coach, Willie McFaul.

World Cup winner Jack Charlton, who took over the United hot seat.

1989

After selling their prized assets – players to become England regulars in Beardsley, Waddle and the emerging Paul Gascoigne – United struggle for survival in the First Division. By the time Newcastle's fate is established, another new boss in Jim Smith is installed at St James Park. United embark on a further spell in Division Two.

1990

Newcastle narrowly miss bouncing straight back to football's elite after a controversial play-off defeat against local rivals Sunderland. Mick Quinn is installed as the Magpies' new centre-forward hero and he nets 34 goals in his first season, including four on his debut against Leeds United.

1991

The pressure to achieve promotion is too much for the Bald Eagle and Jim Smith resigns to be replaced by former Argentinian World Cup winner, Ossie Ardiles. Behind the scenes a share-war for control of the near bankrupt club heats up between the Board and Magpie Group.

1992

Newcastle mark their official centenary year with plenty of headlines as boardroom politics take centre-stage with the partial success of Sir John Hall's take-over bid. With the black'n'whites desperate to avoid relegation to the Third Division for the first time, Ardiles is sacked and Kevin Keegan returns to Gallowgate as the club's saviour.

1993

With Sir John Hall now firmly in control and Keegan installed as a long term manager, United take the football world by storm. Newcastle's finances are transformed off the field, while Keegan develops an entertaining eleven that sweeps the First Division Championship. United's boss also breaks the million pound transfer barrier by paying a record £1.75m for striker Andy Cole.

1994

Newcastle's first season in the Premier League ends with the club in 3rd spot and being branded The Entertainers. Newcastle United quickly become the countries favourite side with their style of gifted, attacking football. Peter Beardsley returns to help Andy Cole fire home a record 41 goals in the season.

1995

With St James Park completely redeveloped into a £25m superstadium, Kevin Keegan shuffles his pack as Andy Cole leaves for Old Trafford in a shock £7m deal that stuns the football scene.

1996

Stars begin to flock to Tyneside as Keegan spends £6m on Les Ferdinand and brings French artiste David Ginola to St James Park. Newcastle's bid for the Premiership Championship is lost at the death to Manchester United. The Magpies had led the table for much of the season, but failed at the last hurdle and finish in Runners-up position.

1997

The disappointment of the previous Title race prompts Newcastle United to revitalise the squad and create a new world record transfer deal when £15m is spent to bring Alan Shearer back to Tyneside. United again bid for the Championship trophy, but in mid-season Kevin Keegan is replaced by Kenny Dalglish and once more the black'n'whites finish in Runners-up spot – this time with a place in the new European Champions League.

1998

Dalglish starts to fashion his own squad, but is rocked by a long term injury to England captain Shearer. Despite this huge set back United taste the Champions League with a notable success over Barcelona before embarking on a run to Wembley in the FA Cup – spearheaded by a near fit Shearer. Newcastle though are second best to the Double winners, Arsenal at Wembley.

1999

Newcastle decide to replace Kenny Dalglish with former Chelsea boss and Dutch master, Ruud Gullit. The former AC Milan ace starts to rebuild the side and United continue to be one of the game's big spenders, purchasing Duncan Ferguson in a £8m deal. Again the Magpies end up at Wembley, once more after another exciting FA Cup run. Alan Shearer scores twice in the semi-final but Newcastle fall to Manchester United – on their way to a celebrated Treble. Off the field a massive £42m ground expansion begins at St James Park.

GEORDIE HEROES

Tyneside loves its hero figures. Newcastle United's history has been packed with a colourful collection of larger than life personalities to have pulled on the black'n'white shirt, characters to have caught the imagination of the club's fanatical support. And none more so in the famous Number 9 shirt. The centre-forward role at St James Park is now a legendary tale. For a century a whole line of famous centre-forwards have donned the black'n'white colours and continually stirred the Geordie crowd. Many dashing, courageous and dynamic players almost out of the Roy of the Rovers comic strip. Each a Geordie hero.

While England skipper and £15m centre-forward Alan Shearer is the present-day hero, over one hundred years ago pioneer Willie Thompson was the first to play in the centre-forward role. Sporting a monster moustache in the fashion of the day, the Northumbrian hit plenty of goals as Newcastle became established as a Football League club. But it was the signing of Glasgow born Jock Peddie that marked the arrival of the Club's first hero figure. The tough Scot arrived on Tyneside late in 1897 from Third Lanark with a reputation for being a free scoring, tearaway leader with a blockbuster shot in either foot. He was big and strong and during a five year stay at Gallowgate netted 78 goals.

Peddie scored most of his goals in the style of the day, a dribbling run with the ball and a ferocious shot to finish. The fans loved it, although alongwith his exploits on the field, he was a temperamental character off it. More than once Jock was in trouble with the Club's directors, often fined for missing training, swearing or indiscipline. It just added to his colourful reputation.

His departure to Manchester United in 1902 was not taken lightly by United's supporters, especially when many months of searching for an adequate replacement came to nothing. The fans demanded another hero figure – as they have done in every decade since. The United committee eventually found their replacement and he was worth waiting for – Bill Appleyard, a 14 stone terror to goalkeepers.

Appleyard arrived in April 1903 from Grimsby Town where he had also worked as a North Sea fisherman. A superb goalpoacher, especially on the right flank, he also aimed to put the goalkeeper in the net as well as the ball – in an era when keepers were unprotected and received some rough treatment from forwards! Appleyard was United's main strike force during the first years of the black'n'whites Edwardian heyday. He scored 88 goals in 146 games and won Championship and FA Cup medals, only narrowly missing an international call-up for England.

Appleyard was forced to quit the top circle due to injury and United plunged into the transfer market in a big way and brought Albert Shepherd to Tyneside in November 1908. Shepherd had been established as Bolton's leader for several years and had also collected England honours. He cost £850, an amount in those days equal to the huge sums paid for current superstars.

Unselfish and astute, Shepherd immediately became a hit with the fans. He was noted for his exciting dashes through the middle and averaged over a goal every second game for the Magpies, scoring 92 in five seasons. A real character, stories abound about his exploits. Once, when barracked by the crowd on a rare off day, he walked off the field as calmly as you like and took no further part in the match! On another occasion, wishing a quick getaway from a fixture, he agreed with the management that if he netted a hat-trick he could leave the field ahead of the whistle – and he did, with three goals to his name!

Like Appleyard, Albert Shepherd won title and cup honours before an injury halted his progress. And by the time Newcastle were ready to start football after the First World War, they needed a new figure to raise the pulse rate on the terrace. That man was Neil Harris who joined the club in May 1920 from Patrick Thistle. Another Glaswegian, his family were noted sportsmen and Harris became a prolific goalscorer for the Magpies, finding the target 101 times. At his peak in 1924, the Scot netted in United's FA Cup victory at Wembley and also led his country's line against England. When reaching the veteran stage, Harris moved onto Notts County, leaving Newcastle to spend heavily once more in the transfer market to bring another hero figure to Tyneside.

The black'n'whites had set their sights on a 5'5" bundle of magic from north of the border who was to become perhaps the greatest figure to appear in a United shirt. Hughie Kilpatrick Gallacher joined the Tynesiders in December 1925 for £6,500, a record fee. He is ranked alongside Dixie Dean as the greatest striker of them all.

One of Newcastle's greatest heroes, Hughie Gallacher.

Hughie could shoot powerfully, head, dribble, create openings, tackle, forage, run all day and often get into trouble with defenders, referees and directors! Goalscoring came naturally. He scored 463 goals at senior level and accumulated 143 for United in only 174 games – including 39 goals in 41 games in season 1926-27 when he skippered Newcastle to the League Championship. Hero-worshipped like no other on Tyneside, Gallacher was often seen in the pubs and clubs of Tyneside mixing with supporters, he was something of a playboy. He loved it. The fans loved it – if Newcastle's directors didn't.

Gallacher controversially moved to Chelsea in 1930 and on his return to Tyneside with the Londoners a record St James Park crowd was established of 68,386 – a mark of his popularity on Tyneside. A regular for the Scotland side, Gallacher later settled in Gateshead and tragically committed suicide in 1957.

Finding a replacement for Hughie Gallacher was impossible and only emphasised United's strange decision to allow him to leave, the Scot having noted at the time he had no wish to travel south. And Newcastle never really found a replacement for years, not until Albert Stubbins came along just before the war. In between several players gave supporters something to cheer, including Jack Allen, a local product from Newburn who arrived at Gallowgate from Sheffield Wednesday. He scored 41 goals in a short but productive stay, including two goals in the 1932 FA Cup final. A young centre-forward from Yorkshire, Jack Smith, did well too. He scored plenty of goals – 73 in 112 matches – but his time at St James Park was clouded with the side's mediocrity in the Second Division.

Tynesider Billy Cairns, bustling and big hearted, had a couple of good seasons and then the war years saw Albert Stubbins rise to prominence as the crowd's favourite. Born in Wallsend, but brought up in the United States, he joined United's juniors in 1937. Developing quickly, he was the nation's top striker during wartime football and grabbed a staggering 237 goals in only 218 games for the Magpies.

Stubbins' firepower and skill were the toast of Tyneside until he joined Liverpool in 1946. Charlie Wayman then took the No 9 shirt for a season before Jackie Milburn was a reluctant replacement. Wor Jackie never wanted to play in the centre-forward's role, but manager George Martin persuaded the former Ashington pit-lad to have a go. And of course he was an instant success.

For the next decade, and for many years after he had left St James Park, Milburn was the fans' darling. Jackie's name immediately revives memories one of the most exciting and thrilling eras in the club's history – lifting the FA Cup three times in five years. In almost 500 games for the Magpies, Jackie netted 239 goals. It is the best on record by any player connected with the Magpies and wasn't so much the colossal number of goals he scored, as the breath-taking manner in which he scored them. Feared for his shooting and speed off the mark, Milburn was first capped in 1949 and went onto play for England 13 times. Playing alongside another huge crowd favourite in left-winger Bobby Mitchell, the pair could do little wrong on Tyneside and were welcomed as royalty wherever they went.

Jackie departed in 1957 and Newcastle had a ready-made replacement to step into both the goalscoring and heroes shoes; Len White. A Yorkshire miner, White slipped into the mould to perfection. At St James Park since arriving in 1953 from Rotherham United, Len netted 153 goals in 270 fixtures with a style that enthralled the fans. Although stocky, he was fast and with classic ball control weaved his way through lines of defenders. All his goals however, couldn't save United from decline and eventual relegation in 1961.

'Wor Jackie', darling of the Geordie crowd for a generation.

Newcastle's period in the Second Division saw Barrie Thomas and Ron McGarry take over the crowd's mantle and the No 9 shirt. Both were characters and Thomas can also claim to have an excellent return of goals – 50 in 78 matches. But for injury his record would have been even better.

The Geordie crowd found a new idol though as flame haired Welshman Wyn Davies arrived at Gallowgate in 1966 for a record fee of £80,000. Davies was never a great goalscorer for the Magpies, but the Welsh international's contribution to the club winning European silverware three years later was enormous. Tough as they come, and able to soak up severe physical battering from defenders, Wyn Davies was the perfect target man and forwards around him like Bryan Robson reeped the benefit. The Tyneside crowd warmed to his battling and never-say-die qualities.

Welsh internationalist Wyn Davies, a powerful centre-forward.

The end of the Davies era came in 1971 and that year saw the beginning of another classic period when another No 9 of special star quality landed on Tyneside. A brash, arrogant 21 year-old, Malcolm Macdonald pulled up at St James Park in a Rolls Royce. Although something of a gamble at a £180,000 fee, manager Joe Harvey's judgement was proved first class. Macdonald's style of play provided United's supporters with thrill a minute action. Macdonald was lightning fast, he had a cracking shot, was strong as a mule and deceivingly good in the air too. Malcolm scored 138 goals in five seasons appearing for England and reaching Wembley twice with the black'n'whites. He was the perfect centre-forward hero. However, a bust up with new manager Gordon Lee saw the Londoner head for Arsenal in 1976 to derision from United's masses.

Malcolm Macdonald, hailed as 'Supermac' by United supporters.

Supermac's departure was a blow and United found it hard to replace his powerplay at centre-forward and they didn't really do so until Mick Quinn and Andy Cole arrived several years later. The fans affection was heeped upon a certain Kevin Keegan in the intervening years, one of United's few non centre-forward hero figures – but probably alongside Gallacher and Milburn the biggest of them all. His arrival in 1982 saw unparalleled euphoria among Newcastle's black'n'white army of supporters. A unique bond between player and fan resulted that hasn't been matched anywhere else in the country.

Once Keegan had departed, Brazilian international centre-forward Mirandinha settled on Tyneside with a big reputation, but failed to live upto the headlines. Then a chirpy scouser by the name of Mick Quinn was signed by manager Jim Smith in 1989. The former Portsmouth striker got off to a marvellous start – the best by any United centre-forward. He netted four goals on his debut against Leeds United and the Mighty Quinn had arrived.

Quinn proceeded to become a lethal finisher in the box and a most popular personality. Only a bad injury saw him loose his place to David Kelly and by the time he was fit again, St James Park was a different place. Kevin Keegan was back and now in charge while Mick was on his way to Coventry City. It was not long before Keegan the manager – and still Keegan the hero too – brought in a centre-forward that the Toon Army immediately responded to. He spent £1.75m on Andy Cole, an almost unknown from Bristol City.

With United in the Premier League the stage was left to Cole the Predator. A total of 68 goals in 84 appearances ensured that the lithe striker became a huge hit with the Geordie public. He broke the club's individual scoring record in season 1993-94 with 41 goals. Many of those goals came with help from another crowd favourite, Peter Beardsley who returned to Gallowgate from Everton. Few players in Newcastle's history have been as popular as the little Geordie who netted so many exceptional goals for the club. But a massive and shock £7m deal with Manchester United broke the partnership and saw Cole move to Old Trafford. The celebrated Toon Army had to wait until the £6m signing of Les Ferdinand before their much needed hero figure had re-appeared.

One of the Premiership's outstanding players, Ferdinand immediately took to the role and found the best form of his career as Newcastle challenged for the Title crown in 1995-96 and 1996-97. Les won the Footballer of the Year Award before moving back to London to join Spurs. And for that latter season, Sir Les, as he was to be nicknamed by the crowd, was to have a partner in attack; Alan Shearer who returned home to Tyneside in a huge fanfare following a world record £15m transfer in the summer of 1996.

The return of Shearer to the club he supported as a kid was just what the Toon Army longed for. If it wasn't a centre-forward hero they loved, it was a local lad made good – Shearer was both. His all round game and professional attitude ensured he became the perfect North East ambassador. And when Les Ferdinand moved on, Duncan Ferguson took over, another big name striker that rapidly gained the respect and following from the supporters. The £8m purchase of the tall and talented Scot from Everton ensured Newcastle fans had still plenty of stars to worship.

Newcastle's record signing at the time, Andy Cole.

The £15 million man, Tyneside-born Alan Shearer.

TOON GLORY

1898: TEST MATCH CONTROVERSY

Newcastle's first taste of football glory took place amidst controversial circumstances. Promotion from the Second Division a century ago was assured only after a series of Test Matches – an early version of the present-day Play-offs. Back in 1898 the top two clubs in Division Two, Burnley and Newcastle United, had to compete against Blackburn Rovers and Stoke of Division One in a mini-league during April to see who would play First Division football.

United began with a 2-1 victory over Stoke, but had star striker Jock Peddie injured. In the return match in the Potteries, Newcastle fell by a single goal and then had to face a double with Blackburn Rovers. At Ewood Park, United were behind 3-1 at the interval, yet battled back into the game during the second period only to loose narrowly by 4-3. The backbone of the side, Tommy Ghee, Jack Ostler and Jimmy Stott at half-back had been outstanding.

That defeat made for an interesting final day. Stoke faced Burnley, a draw of any score would mean both clubs would be in Division One no matter what the result of the United and Rovers clash. To stand any chance Newcastle had to win well and this they did. The Magpies outplayed their Lancashire rivals to win handsomely by 4-0 and supporters rushed to find out the score of the Stoke and Burnley encounter. It was predictably 0-0 and Newcastle's victory was in vain.

However, when full details of the match in the Midlands began to filter north, it was claimed that both Stoke and Burnley had come to an agreement to ensure that a draw was the outcome of the crucial fixture. The Football league took note and scrapped the Test Match results – the system being abolished – and to save any further ill feeling all four clubs were elected into Division One.

Promotion side: (2-3-5) Watts; White, Jackson; Ghee, Ostler, Stott(Capt); Allan(R), Harvey, Peddie, Aitken, Wardrope.
Manager: Director's Committee

1905: CHAMPIONSHIP SHOCK

United's first success at football's premier competition was quite a shock to everyone connected with the game. In the previous season the side had gone through a poor campaign and the transformation that took place for the 1904-05 season was outstanding.

The Magpies' form during November and December gave the club a foundation to make a title bid. As winter approached United played seven games and took full points, a marvellous run that put the black'n'whites at the top of the table. Included was a 6-2 thrashing of reigning champions Sheffield Wednesday. The midfield combination of Alex Gardner, Andy Aitken and Peter McWilliam were at the engine room of the side, while up front, Rutherford, Howie and fearsome centre-forward Bill Appleyard were a handful.

Everton and Manchester City were Tyneside's main rivals for the trophy with April proving the deciding month for all concerned. Newcastle played seven games in that crucial period, losing two but winning the other five, the final three fixtures sealing the race. Newcastle met local rivals Sunderland – at the time something of a jinx club to United – and they lost by 3-1. It was a giant setback with Everton and City looming dangerously.

Newcastle played their final two games away from Gallowgate. The first was at Sheffield Wednesday, and after going a goal behind early on Newcastle left it late to bag three goals and clinch the points. It was on the final day of the season when the destination of the trophy was decided. United needed to win to make sure the championship ended up on Tyneside. They did, in style with a 3-0 victory at Middlesbrough and won the Title by one point from Everton.

Championship side: (2-3-5) Lawrence; McCombie, Carr; Gardner, Aitken(Capt), McWilliam; Rutherford, Howie, Appleyard, Veitch or Orr, Gosnell.
Manager: Directors Committee.

1907: LEAGUE TITLE STROLL

Newcastle opened their second Championship winning season in over 90 degrees, considered the hottest day the game in this country has seen. A record crowd at Gallowgate saw Sunderland defeated 4-2 and from that moment no one could stop United's machine.

The Magpies' home form was outstanding. They won every league fixture on Tyneside until the very last game of the season against Sheffield United. It was in fact The Blades who were one of the clubs to have kept in touch with Newcastle during the Title chase, alongwith Everton and Bristol City. But it was the southwest club from Ashton Gate that pushed the Tynesiders the most. A crucial meeting took place on Easter Saturday. However, Bristol City were no match for the black'n'whites, losing 3-0. That defeat killed off their challenge and the trophy was safe on the St James Park sideboard again.

Newcastle's formation was celebrated the country over. They had a side full of star players like Peter McWilliam and Jimmy Howie, two talented Scottish internationals. And on the flank a Geordie, Jackie Rutherford was a constant source of telling crosses as well as goals. Centre-forward Bill Appleyard, a mountain of a man, proved a menace in the box. United had a tremendous squad of talent. Players already capped or soon to be honoured in United's pool totalled 13 – very few clubs, if any, in that era could boast anywhere close to that.

Championship side: (2-3-5) Lawrence; McCombie or McCracken, Carr; Gardner(Capt), Veitch, McWilliam; Rutherford, Howie, Appleyard or Speedie, Orr or Brown, Gosnell.
Manager: Directors Committee.

Edwardian United.

1909: RECORD DEFEAT INSPIRATION

Newcastle United started the 1908-09 programme almost like a team possessed. They won their first five games and this after a summer of discontent within the dressing-room. Bill Appleyard had departed and his power up front was a big loss by the time the heavy pitches arrived in the winter. His replacement, Bob Blanthorne had tragically broken his leg on his debut, and United's directors needed to find another centre-forward to fill the role. They signed one of the country's best – Bolton's Albert Shepherd.

The England centre-forward's home debut co-incided with the most remarkable fixture to have taken place at St James Park. Newcastle fell to the tune of 9-1 to their biggest foes, Sunderland. It had been an amazing defeat by the Champions elect. Never before, or since, had the Title winners lost so heavily, and on home soil too – and to their sternest of rivals. That Magpie eleven contained several reserves, in for Newcastle's big stars who were out of favour with the directorate at the time. For the next match, the established internationals were back – and how they performed.

That record home defeat acted as an inspiration for the players. As if to show the club directors what they had missed, United couldn't do anything wrong after that fateful day in December. In a spell from that sensational reverse with their Wearside neighbours, to mid April and yet another defeat to Sunderland, United lost only one game. In a run into the New Year they won seven games in a row.

Despite losing key midfielder Alex Gardner to another broken leg, Newcastle came to the crucial make or break stage of the season as leaders. Everton were again Newcastle's main challengers and the Edwardian rivals met at St James Park at Easter. It was the title decider as the Merseysiders had to take full points to stand any chance of overhauling the Magpies. Newcastle didn't let Everton in with a chance and won 3-0 and the black'n'whites went onto create a record haul of points in the First Division.

Championship side: (2-3-5) Lawrence; McCracken, Whitson; Willis, Veitch(Capt), McWilliam; Rutherford, Howie, Shepherd, Stewart, Wilson.
Manager: Directors Committee.

1910: FA CUP GLORY AT LAST

Newcastle had found lifting the elusive FA Cup a trying assignment. Spellbound by the Crystal Palace stadium they had already made four visits to London during the Edwardian era, but on each occasion came away without the trophy (and recorded another unsuccessful trip in 1911). In 1910 they managed a draw against Barnsley, and took their Yorkshire opponents to a replay at Goodison Park where, more at home in the surroundings of Everton's compact stadium, Newcastle found their touch.

Goalmouth action from the 1910 FA Cup Final at Sydenham, in South London.

The Magpies' run to the final started with a hiccup over non-league Stoke. Then in the Southern League, the Potteries club made United battle for everything in the First Round tie that lasted two games. Stoke in fact came very close to causing a huge upset, Newcastle eventually scraping through with a 2-1 victory at St James Park.

Blackburn Rovers and Fulham were comfortably despatched on Tyneside in the next stages of the competition, then Leicester Fosse arrived in the North East and faced a confident United eleven. But the visitors fought gamely and only a late rally saw the Magpies safely through to the semi-final. In the process Newcastle had bagged ten goals and were favourites to reach the final.

Giant-killers Swindon Town faced United in the semi-final. They were a Southern League outfit at the time, but boasted some fine players and unusually for a neutral venue held the advantage, the contest being played at White Hart Lane, only 50 miles from Swindon. The first 45 minutes of the game was an even affair, but in the second period Newcastle were outstanding and dominated their opponents. A snap shot from England winger Jackie Rutherford gave the black'n'whites the lead, then minutes later Jimmy Stewart confirmed the victory with a second.

Centre-forward Albert Shepherd was to be United FA Cup hero that year. A power packed leader, in the cup final replay with Barnsley he was a handful on a wet, greasy surface. Newcastle pounded the Tykes goal during the opening exchanges, but by the interval Barnsley had held out and the contest remained scoreless. In the second-half United made the pressure tell and Shepherd's darting run through the centre – in typical style – gave United the lead with a fast ground shot into the net.

A foul by Barnsley defender Ness led to a penalty and up stepped Shepherd to blast the ball home for what was the first ever spot-kick in a FA Cup final. Newcastle ended up 2-0 winners and the trophy was on its way to Tyneside.

FA Cup winning side: (2-3-5) Lawrence; McCracken, Carr; Veitch(Capt), Low, McWilliam; Rutherford, Howie, Shepherd, Higgins, Wilson.
Manager: Directors Committee.

1924: A TASTE OF WEMBLEY

The new national stadium at Wembley had been opened just one year earlier and the FA Cup now boasted a formidable home, one which was to hold a special magic and to ensure the competition was to become of greater significance in the years to come. Newcastle took to Wembley and its unique atmosphere – in direct contrast to their transfixed displays at the Crystal Palace.

United opened their first run to the famous Twin Towers landmark with a long journey to Portsmouth, a Third Division club thought to be no match for the mighty Newcastle United. But the Magpies found themselves two goals behind at the break. It took a marvellous rally by United to turn the deficit into a 4-2 victory.

The next tie was another difficult encounter – one with Derby County that lasted four thrilling games and stirred passions in both camps as 20 goals were scored. Eventually Newcastle won a classic at St James Park by 5-3, goalgetter in chief Neil Harris striking a hat-trick to turn the match when Derby were in front by two goals.

United's side was full of spirit and character that year. They fielded quality in goalscoring winger Stan Seymour, while the craft came from Scots Willie Gibson and Willie Cowan in midfield. Neil Harris was another from north of the border, he found his goalscoring touch just at the right time.

In Round Five struggling Third Division side Watford faced a confident United eleven, yet in true FA Cup traditions Newcastle didn't get an easy passage in the south. A single goal by Seymour was enough to squeeze the Tynesiders to a meeting with Liverpool on Tyneside. A crowd of over 56,000 witnessed a closely fought 90 minutes of football. Both clubs were evenly matched and United edged through to the semi-final after another 1-0 victory.

Manchester City faced the Magpies in the semi-final at St Andrews in Birmingham and United were rarely troubled. They coasted into the final with a goal from centre-forward Neil Harris in each half.
So to Wembley for the very first time, to the first all ticket cup final and to face old rivals Aston Villa, just above United in the First Division table. It was a final that lived for years. On a soft, wet pitch, Villa started brightly with Magpie stand-in goalkeeper Bill Bradley making good saves. However, as the game progressed United started to take control and began to look dangerous themselves up front.

The deadlock was broken just as many thought extra-time would be needed. Newcastle hit their opponents for two late goals to clinch the trophy. The first was a glorious three man move started in defence and finished with a low drive from just inside the box from Harris. Before anyone had time to settle, Seymour fired home a memorable goal too; collecting a low pass then cutting inside before striking the ball high into the net.

FA Cup winning side: (2-3-5) Bradley; Hampson, Hudspeth(Capt); Mooney, Spencer, Gibson; Low, Cowan, Harris, McDonald, Seymour.
Manager: Directors Committee.

1927: WEE HUGHIE'S CHAMPIONS

Newcastle's directors made a controversial move during the summer of 1926 by appointing the temperamental Scot, Hughie Gallacher as skipper for the new season. Deposing the solid and dependable Frank Hudspeth, it was a decision that reaped dividends as Wee Hughie repaid United with goals and more goals as he led United to the Title trophy.

Gallacher and his Magpie side started off impressively, with a four goal burst over Aston Villa – the 5'5" genius claiming all four goals. He went onto score 36 in only 38 games, the crucial factor behind United's success. With a steady defence marshalled by the veteran Hudspeth and Charles Spencer at centre-half, United's side was a well balanced one with a blend of skilful, yet tough and aggressive football.

The North East was gripped with the Championship race as Sunderland battled for the trophy alongwith United and Huddersfield Town. It was an absorbing contest, which lasted to the very end. Newcastle's home form was exceptional, claiming 19 victories out of 21 played, an all time record which lasted until 1979. And they could always find goals up front. Both Tom McDonald and Stan Seymour were able to strike the net alongside Gallacher – a remarkable feat as the forward line only boasted an average height of 5'6"!

Newcastle met Sunderland and Huddersfield in Championship deciders during March and April. Against their Wearside rivals – second in the table behind United – a new record crowd packed into St James Park to watch the confrontation. A single goal from Gallacher gave United the points and set-up the black'n'whites challenge with Huddersfield Town – team of the era.

Latterly three times Champions in a row, the Yorkshire club was attempting to achieve a unique fourth successive Title win. But on Tyneside it was that man Gallacher who proved to be the difference between the sides. He claimed the only goal of the game, which all but gave the Magpies the Championship trophy. Newcastle claimed the Title with a point in London, at West Ham United. They finished a comfortable five points ahead of Huddersfield – and seven in front of Sunderland.

Championship winning side: (2-3-5) Wilson; Maitland, Hudspeth; Gibson, Spencer, Mackenzie; Urwin, McKay, Gallacher(Capt), McDonald, Seymour.
Manager: Directors Committee.

1932: THE OVER THE LINE FINAL

When Newcastle started out on their 1932 FA Cup run to Wembley no-one envisaged what a storm would blow up after the trophy was in the hands of skipper Jimmy Nelson. The now infamous disputed goal netted by Jack Allen against Arsenal is still debated fiercely to this day – perhaps the most controversial goal in the history of the competition.

The black'n'whites took care of both Blackpool and Southport in the early rounds of the tournament, thrashing Southport 9-0 in a replay at Hillsborough – the club's record FA Cup score. In the Fifth Round, relegation threatened Leicester City arrived at St James Park and took an early lead only for the Magpies to fight back and win 3-1 with United's dynamo in midfield, Sammy Weaver having a marvellous 90 minutes. Alongwith England man Weaver, United's side relied on the prompting of inside-forwards Jimmy Richardson and Harry McMenemy, two schemers of marvellous quality.

Watford faced Newcastle in the next round, a club that had upset other giants that year. But the minnows were given a football lesson as Newcastle cruised home by 5-0. United gave an exhibition of football and also hit the woodwork twice. Centre-forward Jack Allen crashed home a hat-trick.

Semi-final opponents Chelsea were aiming to make it an all London final with Arsenal being in the other half of the draw. They included in their line up several star names and former Magpie crowd hero, Hughie Gallacher. While al1 eyes were on the Scots ace, United efficiently took care of the Cockneys in the first half-hour of the match. A Lang free-kick was headed goalwards by Allen and when his effort hit the woodwork the Newcastle leader reacted the quickest to strike a low drive into the net.

Jimmy Boyd then went on a tricky run going past two defenders to send in a telling cross for his opposite winger, Tommy Lang to head in from close range. Gallacher did pull a goal back for Chelsea in that torrid opening first forty-five minutes of play, but United held on after the interval and could thank England international goalkeeper Albert McInroy for several fine stops.

The team of the era, Arsenal, faced Newcastle at Wembley. Dominating influence throughout the Thirties decade, the Gunners fielded a star-studded line-up and on paper were far superior to United's eleven. They had enough talent to swamp the Magpies. Yet Newcastle's formidable team spirit was a key factor, while the black'n'whites also had lady luck on their side.

A classic final resulted which saw fast flowing, end to end football captivate the crowd. As expected Arsenal looked the better side early on and took the lead through Bob John after McInroy and Nelson had misjudged a cross. Newcastle though came back strongly and went close on several occasions. Then it happened, the talking point for weeks, months and years to come.

In the 38th minute Dave Davidson intercepted a Hapgood pass and sent a long through ball for Jimmy Richardson to chase on the right wing. The United player stretched for the ball and wipped in a cross before – or as he thought – the ball went out of play on the goal line. As the Arsenal defence relaxed for a split second waiting for a goal-kick decision, in flashed Jack Allen to drive the ball into the net for the equaliser. Referee Percy Harper awarded a goal and United were level at 1-1.

It was not until after the game that a rumpus started. Press photos and newsreel film appeared to show the ball out of play. Mr Harper said adamantly, "It was a goal. As God is my judge the man was in play". Importantly he did not say, the ball was in play!

United were back in the match and went from strength to strength. In the second period they were the better side and penned the Londoners back and eventually grabbed the winning goal when Jack Allen slipped past two defenders before hitting the ball into the net off a post.

FA Cup winning side: (2-3-5) McInroy; Nelson(Capt), Fairhurst; Mackenzie, Davidson, Weaver; Boyd, Richardson, Allen, McMenemy, Lang.
Manager: Andy Cunningham.

1948: PROMOTION BOOM

Football after the close of the Second World War boomed. Supporters flocked to watch the game now that peace was restored and Newcastle United were the best supported club in the country with regular attendances of over 50,000 at every home game. All they needed was First Division football. In season 1947-48 the Magpies' side containing a blend of home-grown talent and expensive signings, made a sustained bid to get back into the highest level of the Football League.

By the opening weeks of 1948, Newcastle had climbed into 3rd place but had to rid themselves of their inconsistency if they were to seriously challenge for a promotion place. At times the Magpies could play some tremendous football with skilful players like Len Shackleton and TommyPearson pulling the strings for Milburn up front. But they had to learn to scrap as well. Manager George Martin changed his team midway through the season, selling classy ball-players Shackleton and Pearson, and bringing in Norman Dodgin and George Stobbart, two gritty performers. With the likes of Brennan and Harvey, Newcastle's side now had battling qualities.

With that massive home support, Newcastle had almost a goal start at every match on Tyneside and kept in touch at the top of the table where Birmingham City were favourite to lift the Second Division Championship. The second spot rested between three clubs; United, Sheffield Wednesday and Southampton.

The crunch came in April. United faced Fulham at St James Park and grabbed both points with a late penalty after Milburn had been tripped in the box. George Stobbart struck the spot-kick well and scored. Three days later Sheffield Wednesday faced United at Gallowgate. The points at stake meant virtual promotion to both clubs and in a cracker of a match United won 4-2 after being behind to the Yorkshire club. St James Park was packed with 66,483 and witnessed an epic, Frank Houghton netting the crucial goals in the closing, dramatic minutes with the match standing in stalemate at 2-2.

On FA Cup final day United visited White Hart Lane where they secured the mathematical point required for promotion with a 1-1 draw. After 14 years in the wilderness, the black'n'whites were back in the First Division.

Promotion winning side: (2-3-5) Fairbrother; Cowell or Fraser, Craig; Harvey(Capt), Brennan, Dodgin; Sibley, Stobbart, Milburn, Shackleton, Pearson.
Manager: George Martin.

1951: WOR JACKIE'S DOUBLE

United's side of the Fifties decade has gone down in history as one of the finest of all cup sides, winning the FA Cup on three occasions inside five years between 1951 and 1955. Their remarkable run commenced with a tie against Bury and United romped home 4-1. But after that Newcastle faced two difficult hurdles, firstly a home match against Bolton Wanderers. A 67,596 crowd – the biggest crowd at St James Park in post-war football – saw a game swamped with thrills and action. Newcastle went in front, only for Bolton to take a 2-1 lead, then Jackie Milburn stamped his presence on the match to net twice and give United victory by 3-2.

Milburn was Newcastle's dangerman. Alongwith Bobby Mitchell and George Robledo, the black'n'white's attack was potent and Newcastle soon became a popular side around the country. In Round Five, United's trip to Stoke ended with another entertaining cup-tie that Newcastle won 4-2. And Third Division outfit Bristol Rovers were eliminated, but not until the Magpies had been given a torrid time in a tie that went to a replay.

Newcastle faced Midland club Wolves in the semi-final at Hillsborough. Despite a 0-0 scoreline a thrilling game took place. The referee disallowed two goals within four minutes of the start – one for each side – and thereafter United missed a hatful of chances. In the replay at Leeds Road, Huddersfield, another absorbing contest took place. Two goals for Newcastle inside a minute with Wolves leading and threatening to run the Magpies off their feet, put the Geordies into their eighth FA Cup final. United just about deserved the victory in a close tussle. Milburn and Mitchell were the stars to find the net, two names to figure time and time again during this era of FA Cup glory.

Blackpool were the black'n'whites opponents in the final. And Newcastle were not the fancied club as the whole nation wanted a Stanley Matthews cup win. It was in fact an evenly balanced contest; United were in 4th place in the First Division table while Blackpool were 2nd. But it was Newcastle who clicked on the day – and Milburn and not Matthews who grabbed the headlines.

Wor Jackie inspired the Magpies. Almost unaided he struck two superb goals in a five minute spell mid-way through the second half to lift the trophy for United. Firstly he beat the Blackpool offside trap to sprint clear and net, then struck a magnificent long range effort into the top corner of the net after sparkling approach play involving a cheeky back-heel from Ernie Taylor. It was one of the best ever goals scored on the Wembley turf. Milburn had scored in every round of the competition and deserved the accolade that followed.

FA Cup winning side: (2-3-5) Fairbrother; Cowell, Corbett; Harvey(Capt), Brennan, Crowe; Walker, Taylor, Milburn, Robledo(G), Mitchell.
Manager: Stan Seymour.

1952: TOUGH ROUTE TO GLORY

Without doubt 1952 was Newcastle's hardest route to Wembley. They faced four clubs out of the top six in the First Division and had only one home tie. However, the Magpies feared no one, they fielded a cup side packed with spirit, quality and match-winners. And in the opening tie against Aston Villa at St James Park they showed everyone they were aiming for a successive Wembley appearance.

Villa raced to a 2-0 lead within 13 minutes of the match as Newcastle made a dreadful start in their defence of the FA Cup. But United's side never gave up and had a reputation for being at their most dangerous with the odds against them. Foulkes pulled a goal back, however Villa seemed to be holding on for a memorable victory with only eight minutes left on the referee's watch. Then Scottish international winger Bobby Mitchell took over when all seemed lost. He scored two goals in the space of seconds with spectacular shots to put United 3-2 ahead. And Bobby Dazzler, as he was nicknamed, made another goal for George Robledo and Villa left the field shell-shocked.

That superb win put United face to face with Title holders Tottenham Hotspur at White Hart Lane, a draw as tough as they come. An epic struggle was expected and in front of nearly 70,000 in North London, United destroyed the country's top side by 3-0, with Mitchell again proving the matchwinner. Newcastle had another long trip in Round Five, to Swansea where the black'n'whites managed a 1-0 win after a gruelling contest.

Yet another difficult game followed, and another long trek for the Tynesiders. This time high riding Portsmouth, twice Champions in the era, faced United and another classic cup-tie resulted. United won through 4-2 thanks to a marvellous and much celebrated Jackie Milburn hat-trick.

So to another semi-final at Hillsborough and a meeting with Blackburn Rovers. A dour, tense and scoreless match took place, United being out of sorts, but Rovers were unable to capitalise on Newcastle's lack of form. It was though a different story in the replay at Elland Road. The Magpies played much better and should have been three goals up at half-time, but United fans had to wait until the second period for the incisive points of the game. A Milburn cross was headed home by George Robledo only for Rovers to quickly equalise. And a place in the FA Cup final was decided by a crucial penalty-kick in the dying minutes. A Robledo header was handled on the line and up stepped Bobby Mitchell to blast United to Wembley.

Old cup final rivals Arsenal – going for the Double that year – met United at the Twin Towers. United fielded the same team that had competed in all the other games during the cup run, and in a final that never rose to great heights a solitary goal from George Robledo was enough to keep the trophy on Tyneside for another year. After the Gunners had been reduced to ten men through an injury to Wally Barnes, Magpie winger Bobby Mitchell went on a typical mazy run on his flank before looping over a cross to the far post for Robledo to head into the net off a post for a late winning goal.

FA Cup winning side: (2-3-5) Simpson; Cowell, McMichael; Harvey(Capt), Brennan, Robledo(E); Walker, Foulkes, Milburn, Robledo(G), Mitchell.
Manager: Stan Seymour.

1955: WEMBLEY TREBLE

United's side in 1955 was an inconsistent and unpredictable eleven. Few judges reckoned they were good enough to lift the trophy that year, but possessing an uncompromising skipper in Jimmy Scoular, the Magpies astounded everyone – even some of their own supporters. Plymouth Argyle proved difficult opponents to overcome in the Third Round clash but a goal from Vic Keeble saw the Geordies through to another potentially giantkilling tie with Brentford. And once more a typical cup-tie was in store as the lower division side matched United's superior technique with effort and spirit. But Newcastle gained a 3-2 victory and then faced a long contest with Nottingham Forest.

Jimmy Scoular holds The FA Cup aloft on United's return to Gallowgate in 1955.

Forest were dominant at the City Ground and United appeared to be heading for a knock-out until Jackie Milburn squeezed home an equaliser in the dying moments of the match. The first replay was postponed due to frost and snow, and at the second attempt Forest put up a great fight at St James Park, pushing the tie into extra-time and claiming a 2-2 draw. So to a third meeting, and at Gallowgate reserve striker Alan Monkhouse claimed two goals to give United the victory.

In the quarter-final, Huddersfield Town proved also troublesome opponents. Newcastle had a narrow escape in Yorkshire, earning a replay with another late equaliser, while on Tyneside the Magpies needed extra-time to progress to the semi-final with a 2-0 win.

Giant-killers York City — from the Third Division — faced United and the black'n'whites very nearly allowed the minnows to go through to Wembley. The Yorkshire club deserved their 1-1 draw, but had missed their chance as United gave a much more polished display in the replay at Roker Park, winning 2-0.

Newcastle's third FA Cup final in the space of five years – a rare feat upto then – was against a skilled Manchester City eleven marshalled by Don Revie and his famous Revie plan. They had put a stop to Sunderland and the first Tyne-Wear final, but couldn't halt the Magpies. With Scoular a dominant force in midfield, and Mitchell causing havoc on the flank – especially when City were reduced to ten men following an injury to Meadows – Newcastle ended comfortable winners by 3-1. Jackie Milburn made headlines again by scoring inside the first minute, then the quickest goal at Wembley. Mitchell and George Hannah recorded the Magpies' other strikes.

FA Cup winning side: (2-3-5) Simpson; Cowell, Batty; Scoular(Capt), Stokoe, Casey; White, Milburn, Keeble, Hannah, Mitchell.
Manager: Duggie Livingstone.

1965: HARVEY'S SPIRIT

Having witnessed local rivals Sunderland promoted into the First Division the year before, United fans were desperate to see Newcastle follow the Wearside lead. The year started badly for the Magpies though, losing Alan Suddick, the side's young Under 23 international star, with a knee injury. But Joe Harvey had built a solid and spirited combination and despite lacking Suddick's flair and vision, Newcastle became favourites for the Second Division trophy relying on a solid and settled defence with Jim Iley, John McGrath and Stan Anderson forming the backbone of the side.

Newcastle climbed to top of the table by mid September then dipped to 6th place, but as winter approached the black'n'whites clicked, logging seven wins in a row. Included was a 5-0 thrashing of promotion rivals Northampton Town and a Christmas double over Middlesbrough. At the turn of the year they stood firmly at the head of the division.

February was however a bad month for the Tynesiders. United didn't pick up full points at all and lost top spot to the Cobblers which shook confidence. Norwich City and Bolton were also closing the gap on the Magpies too. A 2-1 victory at Portsmouth was much needed to restore hope, then an important win over rivals Norwich was recorded which took United back into the leader's position.

The deciding contest took place on Good Friday against Bolton Wanderers and a huge holiday crowd of almost 60,000 saw the black'n'whites record a 2-0 victory after a hard fought tussle with a Bolton side also pushing for a promotion place. A potent shot from Jim Iley from the edge of the box put the Geordies on their way and on the final whistle United found themselves back in Division One. All that was left now was to secure the Championship trophy. This was achieved with three draws as the side wound down after the Bolton climax.

Promotion winning side: (2-3-5) Marshall; Craig, Clark; Anderson(Capt), McGrath, Iley; Hockey or Robson, Hilley, McGarry or Cummings, Penman, Suddick.
Manager: Joe Harvey.

1969: THE HIGHWAYS OF EUROPE

When Newcastle started the 1968-69 European campaign in the Inter Cities Fairs Cup – the forerunner of the UEFA Cup – jetting the airways of Europe was something completely new for the North East region. And how the club, and public, enjoyed it. Thrills and incident followed month after month as remarkably United went all the way to the final in their first season of European football.

The Magpies started their European adventure with an attractive tie against Dutch giants Feyenoord. United were given little chance by anyone outside Tyneside, yet in no uncertain terms the Geordies showed that this spirited and hard working United side were going to be no pushovers and not just in the competition to make up the numbers.

A crowd of over 46,000 saw the big names of Dutch football given a football lesson as Newcastle recorded a creditable 4-0 victory, one that could easily have turned into a thrashing as the woodwork saved Feyenoord on no less than three occasions.

With big Welsh centre-forward Wyn Davies proving a handful for European defences and his striking partner Bryan Robson always around to pick up the pieces, United found they had an attacking solution that was hard to counter. And with captain Bob Moncur, after recovering from injury, marshalling the defence, Newcastle started to surprise many in the tournament.

Next came two more seasoned European clubs; Sporting Lisbon and Real Zaragoza. And each side felt the force of Newcastle's striking duo of Davies and Robson. Both games were close matches over the two legs but Newcastle squeezed through to meet Portuguese novices Vittoria Setubal. They were crushed 5-1 on Tyneside, on an evening the heavens opened with snow to give United a distinct advantage.

That success took United into the semi-final and an all British momentous clash with Glasgow Rangers – a tie that just about had everything. At Ibrox, a crowd of 75,580 saw a characteristic dogged display from the black'n'whites, earning a 0-0 draw with keeper Willie McFaul saving a spot-kick. The return leg was full of drama and tension. Newcastle raced to a 2-0 lead when the thousands of visiting Scots' fans in the 60,000 crowd invaded the pitch in a bid to get the match cancelled. They failed, although the scenes had repercussion for Rangers over the immediate years, and the Magpies were through to their first European final.

Tyneside's European champions in 1969.

Waiting for the Geordie newcomers were one of Europe's top sides at the time, Hungarians Ujpesti Dosza. Again few gave Newcastle much of a chance, but in the first leg the black'n'whites secured a 3-0 lead with skipper Bob Moncur striking two goals. In Budapest, Ujpesti showed how good a side they were in the opening 45 minutes and pulled back two goals by the interval. United needed to dig deep and get back in the final. This they did in an amazing second-half display, scoring three times to win the trophy 6-2 on aggregate.

Fairs Cup winning side: (4-3-3) McFaul; Craig, Burton, Moncur(Capt), Clark; Gibb, Arentoft, Scott; Davies, Robson, Sinclair. Sub: Foggon.
Manager: Joe Harvey.

1984: KEEGAN MANIA

United needed inspiration as the Eighties decade opened. Newcastle had slipped into Division Two and struggled to press for a promotion place. That inspiration arrived in the shape of former England captain Kevin Keegan who landed on Tyneside amidst jubilant scenes during the summer of 1982. Keegan transformed an average side into a distinguished one and for the 1983-84 season he led the side back to Division One in a much celebrated season full of attacking and flamboyant football.

The big four clubs in the Second Division at the time; United alongwith Manchester City, Sheffield Wednesday and Chelsea contested the three promotion places throughout the programme. At the half-way stage of the season the Magpies were in 3rd place and by the time they played Portsmouth at Fratton Park were starting to hit form. United won 4-1 and the black'n'whites sensational front trio of Chris Waddle and Peter Beardsley, backed and prompted by the talent of Keegan, were the difference between the black'n'whites and the rest. The threesome went onto collect 65 goals, many goals of absolute quality included.

An important victory at Maine Road over Manchester City soon followed and over Easter, United sealed their place in the top three by walloping Carlisle – who had made a late push for promotion – 5-1 and then gaining three points by defeating Derby County 4-0. Although mathematically they still needed a point, the celebrations started and the chant of Keegan – Keegan echoed around Tyneside. United went to Huddersfield Town and despite being two goals behind clawed themselves back with two stunning strikes from Beardsley and Mills and gained a place in Division One.

Kevin Keegan, who inspired the black 'n' whites in 1983-84.

Promotion winning side: (4-4-3) Thomas or Carr; Anderson, Carney, Roeder, Wharton or Ryan; McCreery, McDermott, Wharton or Trewick; Beardsley, Keegan(Capt), Waddle.
Manager: Arthur Cox.

1993: THE MESSIAH RETURNS

With the Magpies at the centre of a rapid and monumental transformation led by Sir John Hall, Kevin Keegan – this time as manager — had the job of getting the club into the money-spinning Premier League – and quickly. Keegan's return as boss was heralded as a new coming and Newcastle United's fortunes never looked back.

The Tynesiders opened the 1992-93 season with high hopes, yet no one – even Keegan – expected the start they would make. The Magpies won ten games out of ten from the big kick-off and romped to the top of the table. They were headline news – and achieved in a stylish, charismatic manner. Newcastle claimed 11 wins in a row with a victory at Roker Park over Sunderland, then faltered at home to Grimsby, just when the all time league record was about to be claimed.

United stuttered after their incredible start, but rarely looked likely to be knocked off their top spot perch. Up front David Kelly and Gavin Peacock formed a good partnership, while in defence Barry Venison and Steve Howey held things firm. And youngster Lee Clark was hailed as the new local hero in midfield. Keegan was also not afraid to buy big in the transfer market to make sure the Magpies claimed the Championship. He brought in Rob Lee and Andy Cole – for a record £1.75m – as well as others to cement his squad.

After slipping a touch over the winter, Newcastle raised their game as spring approached and the sunshine conditions suited their free flowing brand of football. A tense derby meeting with local rivals Sunderland marked the promotion run-in and a single goal direct from a free-kick from one of Keegan's new men, Scott Sellars put the club on the right track. A fixture against Grimsby Town in Cleethorpes was to take United into the Premier League. A Tyneside invasion of the coastal town witnessed goals from Andy Cole and David Kelly launch United into the big-time. United celebrated with a 7-1 thrashing of Leicester City on the last day of the season, a remarkable match which saw United 6-0 up at half-time after a scintillating display. The Toon Army had been born and they partied for many a day afterwards.

Promotion winning side: (4-4-2) Srnicek; Venison(Capt), Howey, Scott, Beresford; Lee, Bracewell or O'Brien, Clark, Sheedy or Sellars; Kelly, Cole or Peacock.
Manager: Kevin Keegan.

CONTINENTAL MAGS

Football in the United Kingdom has changed dramatically over the last decade, especially so during the last five years. One of the most striking differences on the domestic game has been the influx of players from the Continent and further afield in South America. For almost a century British football only saw a sprinkling of foreign stars grace the turf, now every top club has players representing a multitude of different countries, including some of the world's most talented players.

Until recently Newcastle United had fielded very few personalities from a far. However, one of the very best goalscorers in English post-war football hailed from South America and he served the Magpies with distinction earning a special bond with United's fans. George Robledo was the clubs first foreign signing. Born in Chile of an English mother, the stocky inside-forward come striker moved to Tyneside from Barnsley in January 1949 alongwith his younger brother Ted for a £23,000 fee. Already a noted goalscorer when he headed for Tyneside, Robledo's partnership with Jackie Milburn saw his career take-off. A grafter for the ball, Robledo had the eye for a chance and struck the ball hard and true whenever an opportunity developed.

The Chilean hit 91 goals for United in 166 games, including a record equalling 39 in season 1951-52 and many crucial efforts during the Magpies' runs to Wembley in 1951 and 1952. George struck the winning goal in the final showdown with Arsenal, a far post header that crept into the net off the post. Back home in Chile he was a hero figure pulling on his country's jersey during the 1950 World Cup when he faced an England side in Brazil.

Robledo left Tyneside alongwith his brother to return to Chile in May 1953 and the club had a long wait before another continental created such a bond with supporters. On the fringe of the side was Bermuda born full-back Arnold Woollard during the Fifties, while Dane Benny Arentoft pulled on the black'n'white shirt from 1969 to 1971. He arrived from Morton and served the black'n'whites well in a short period on Tyneside. A midfield worker, Arentoft had a key role to play as United lifted the Inter Cities Fairs Cup in 1969 and found himself on the scoresheet in the final over Ujpesti. But Benny didn't stay long thereafter moving to Blackburn Rovers and in 1980 Tyneside witnessed the unveiling of their first Dutchman, midfielder Frans Koenen. Possessing a neat touch on the ball, Koenen never came to terms with the rigours of the English Second Division and returned to Holland within a year.

With the club being heavily criticised over the sale of star players like Waddle and Beardsley, Newcastle's manager of the time Willie McFaul attempted to rekindle spirits by bringing the first Brazilian to England when the black'n'whites signed international centre-forward Mirandinha in August 1987 for £575,000. The deal was headline news and the record signing put United – and Mira – into the spotlight. But his Brazilian skills were no place for a relegation dogfight and only briefly did English spectators witness any South American magic.

During the 1988-89 season, with United struggling and Jim Smith new to the manager's position, two more Danish players arrived on Tyneside, Frank Pingel and Benny Kristensen. At one stage United fielded a novel twin attack of Brazilian, Mirandinha and Dane, Pingel. That did not work and with the Brazilian moving on after 24 goals in 69 games, Pingel attempted to make an impression. An honest and hardworking striker, he never made the grade on Tyneside but later developed into an international

Chilean striker George Robledo, who won two FA Cup medals with United.

striker after impressing in the Bundesliga. His Danish colleague Kristensen however, did make a good impression in a black'n'white shirt. A central defender with craft and the ability to move forward from the back line, Benny was already one of Denmark's top performers when he joined the United set-up in 1989 having won league and cup honours with Aarhus. Winning 20 caps for his country, a bad knee injury stopped Kristensen from challenging for a place in the Kevin Keegan led resurgence at St James Park.

Another of Jim Smith's continental signings who did become one of Keegan's men, was goalkeeper Pavel Srnicek who landed on Tyneside as very much a raw talent on trial in December 1990. The Czech keeper was at that stage of his career very much a novice and could speak little English. But the likeable Srnicek developed into a first class goalkeeper who formed a strong player-fan relationship with the Toon Army. He had his ups and downs with Kevin Keegan and ultimately was to bitterly fall out with Kenny Dalglish, but many Newcastle supporters maintain he was the pick of United's goalkeepers during the nineties decade.

Kevin Keegan's management heralded the modern invasion of continental stars to Tyneside. Nicos Papavasiliou was Special K's first signing in 1993. The Cypriot international looked good in midfield to start with, but faded quickly. Then Keegan was impressed with the form of Belgium's Philippe Albert and Switzerland's Marc Hottiger during the World Cup in the USA in 1994. The arrival of Albert, an experienced and classy defender from Anderlecht, marked for the first time since the days of George Robledo, a player of real foreign quality to be housed at Gallowgate.

Costing United £2.65m in August 1994, Albert's appearance co-incided with Newcastle's newly found Premier League status and Entertainers tag. He was a defender who could attack with menace and often found himself scoring goals for the Magpies.

A year later another Keegan continental signing made a huge impression. The £2.5m purchase of David Ginola from Paris St Germain during the summer of 1995 was an inspirational deal and set United's fanatical Toon Army alight with expectation. Born on the Mediterranean coast, Ginola

French artiste David Ginola delighted The Toon Army.

came to Tyneside as a player of experience, like Albert, having reached three European semi-finals, including the Champions Cup in 1994-95. Ginola was a virtuoso of the tallest order in midfield or on the wing and rapidly made a huge impression on Tyneside public and the wider English game. With the likes of Ginola and Albert at the heart of Kevin Keegan's side, United aimed for the Premier League title – and very nearly succeeded.

And Keegan was not going to stop there. The Newcastle boss broke the club record transfer by bringing Colombia's exciting striker Tino Asprilla to the North East when he joined Newcastle in a £7.5m deal from Italian club Parma in February 1996. Another player of exceptional talent, yet one at times to infuriate with his inconsistency, Asprilla was another headline maker. He rarely performed week in, week out in domestic action, but was a real matchwinner on the European stage where the continental style of play was more suited to his game. But his overall games and goals record of 18 in 62 appearances for United before he returned to Parma was a disappointment.

Managers soon found that they could purchase international players from abroad at a much reduced transfer fee compared to homegrown talent. Kenny Dalglish brought in many new faces from around Europe. United also took advantage of the new Bosman ruling to bring Georgian international Temuri Ketsbaia to Tyneside from Greece in June 1997. The tricky striker or midfielder has proved a popular character in Newcastle, always capable of a flash of genius that will lead to a goal.

Dalglish also raided Greece for two other internationals in Nikos Dabizas and George Geogiadis, both regulars for their country. Dabizas cost United £1.3m from Olympiakos and looked to be a solid centre-half, especially after his display in the 1998 FA Cup semi-final against Sheffield United shortly after his arrival. But his 1998-99 form was a disappointment, while his fellow countryman Georgiadis was rarely given an opportunity. United's boss also tried unsuccessfully with Bjarni Gudjonnson of Iceland, Germany's Ralf Kiedel and David Terrier of France.

John Dahl Tomasson was rated highly when he joined United's set-up in July 1997 from Dutch club Heerenven. The young Dane cost £2.20m, but his introduction to English football did not go as planned and he moved to Feyenoord after a single season at Gallowgate. Another player to have found the English game difficult to adapt to is Italian Alessandro Pistoni, who cost United £4.30m when Dalglish brought him to Tyneside from Inter Milan in July 1997. An expensive signing, the former Italian Under 21 international full-back started well in a black'n'white shirt, but injury and loss of form saw him at one point loaned back to Seria A.

Andreas Andersson was also signed from top Italian football – this time from AC Milan – after Kenny Dalglish had been impressed with his development with Gothenburg. A Swedish international, Andersson cost United £3m, but has yet to capture the form up front that prompted, both United and Milan, to invest heavily in his talent.

Following the France 98 World Cup, Newcastle plunged for two of the tournaments star players. Included was a World Cup winner in French striker Stephan Guivarch'h who joined Dalglish's growing band of continental talent at St James Park. Guivarc'h cost Newcastle £3.5m from Auxerre after proving that in French football he had a goals record second to none. But Guivarc'h arrived on Tyneside having impressed little on the world stage, and he was not to impress in the Premier League either, moving very swifty to Ibrox, joining Glasgow Rangers for a similar fee.

Tino Asprilla proved to be a wonderful player in European football.

One of Dalglish's better continental signings was German midfield ace Dietmar Hamann who had emerged from France 98 as a talented linkman. The tall and lithe Bavarian signed for United from Bayern Munich in July 1998 for a £4.5m fee and after a tentative start began to stamp his authority on the Premiership with a series of assured displays from midfield. Possessing a terrific shot, Hamann's use of the long and short ball became key in United's tactical plan before his move to Liverpool in 1999.

Another player in midfield to have become a favourite of black'n'white supporters is Nol Solano, the first Peruvian to play in England. Landing on Tyneside from Argentinean club Boca Juniors for a £3m fee in August 1998, Solano has a silky touch on the ball and, like Hamann, can hit the ball with venom. A regular for his country Peru, Solano enjoyed a good first season in the Premier League.

Kenny Dalglish's continental spending spree also saw Frenchman Laurent Charvet settle in the North East, a former Cannes and Chelsea defender, he joined ex Sunderland keeper and fellow Frenchman Lional Perez at Gallowgate.

When Dalglish was replaced by Ruud Gullit, himself one of the first top managers from abroad to arrive in England, the continental trend continued. The former Dutch international player was soon on the look out all over Europe for quality players to replace some of his predecessors buys. In came young French full-back from Paris St Germain, Didier Domi for £3.25m in December 1998, while Croatia Zagreb's Silvio Maric arrived two months later for a £3.65m fee. Both were young and highly rated on the continent. So to was Louis Saha, another Frenchman who claimed a loan deal from Metz during the 1998-99 season.

During the close season of 1999 Ruud Gullit swung into action again, signing three experienced defenders. He went back to Paris St Germain to capture French international centre-half Alain Goma for £4.75m then completed the signing of Franck Dumas of Monaco. United's first Spanish player and another defender on the international stage, Elena Marcelino from Mallorca, joined the club for a fee of over £5m.

With the wider freedom of Europe now very much part of life in the United Kingdom, continental players are here to stay. They certainly add an extra dimension to the British game.

Peruvian Nol Solano, one of the latest of the club's international signings.

ST JAMES PARK

The new Millennium will see Newcastle United's famous home of St James Park transformed into a towering structure, a stadium to house 51,000 supporters with facilities the envy of most clubs in Europe. It will be a super-stadium fit for the Millennium, the zenith of a redevelopment project lasting almost a decade, and a fitting conclusion to what has been at times a highly controversial issue on Tyneside that has seen feuds simmer and explode during the past 75 years.

The story of the development of Newcastle United's traditional headquarters on the edge of the city centre has been one of much intrigue featuring intense local politics over the years. It has been a talking point in the region for generations, and even at one stage led to words being spoken in the House of Commons. Newcastle United have – as tenants of the prestigious site – never had an easy route from the outset in attempting to modernise their facilities. And with a relationship between the City Council landlord and football club more at home in the era of the Cold War for much of United's history, controversy and confrontation was the name of the game until recently.

St James Park is the oldest football stadium in the North East, and now with both Roker Park and Ayresome Park disappearing from the map, is also the traditional home of the game. Football was first played on the St James Park turf as early as 1880 and has been the home of three clubs; Newcastle Rangers, Newcastle West End and Newcastle East End who moved to the arena in the summer of 1892 shortly before changing their name to Newcastle United.

Situated on a small hill overlooking the city and part of the historic Town Moor owned by the Freemen of the City – which further complicated any development proposals – St James Park is very close to the spot of the city's execution gallows, the last hanging taking place in 1844, less than 40 years before football was first played in the vicinity.

Back in Victorian Tyneside, St James Park was barely a rough patch of grazing land and had a notorious slope, a drop of fully 18 feet from the north to south goal. Local butchers could still graze their animals on the pitch before being led to slaughter! The ground was bounded by Leazes Park and the exquisite Georgian Leazes Terrace, built to house some of the elegant ladies and gents of Tyneside. While the classical architectural features of Leazes Terrace provided a magnificent backdrop to the arena, it would in the future cause the Club untold difficulties in trying to develop stands around such a historic and listed building.

By the time Newcastle East End had been installed at St James Park development had only been completed in a minor way. And when Newcastle United started to take part in Football League action a small stand had been erected, but local residents were soon complaining to the Town Clerk and threatened to take legal proceedings to stop the "intolerable nuisance" of playing football!

With Newcastle United's promotion to the First Division in 1898, the club made a big effort to start to develop the ground. However, approvals from the local corporation came very slowly and in February 1899 it was recorded that the club were even prepared to move from the site because of the poor state of the pitch and accommodation. Major building work eventually started though, with a new stand at the Gallowgate End being erected, the pitch being levelled and relayed and a terrace formed on the other sides of the ground. A corrugated iron fence enclosed the ground and the capacity was announced at 30,000.

A much bigger and grandiose development plan was put in to action only 5 years later when a complete reconstruction of the ground took place. United's growing stature – they were to win three Championships in the coming years – prompted the club to think and act big. From a modest 30,000 arena United soon opened what was classed as the best stadium in the country at the time, one to house upwards of 60,000. A huge new stand was erected on the Barrack Road side of the ground and substantial terraces formed on the remaining three sides of the ground. Also built was a vast swimming pool beneath the stand with player's facilities, a luxury touch the envy of every club in the Football League. The new stadium was opened in September 1905 with pomp and ceremony. Tyneside at the time had a stadium to be proud of – however one that remained largely unaltered for the next 70 years as further development plans were constantly thwarted.

During the Twenties decade the club attempted to take development a stage further, putting plans together for covered accommodation on the open sides of the ground. Archibald Leitch, a distinguished football ground architect was employed to produce a scheme which included double-decker stands and complete cover around the ground. However, after much wrangling between landlord and planners which lasted to 1930, all that was built was a modest roof over the Leazes End enclosure.

Immediately after World War Two, the club's board again attempted to erect a stand on the Leazes Terrace side of the ground but could not come to any agreement. And during the Fifties United's officials were again in turbulent disagreement with the Council over the thorny question of developing the same side of the stadium. United applied to build a two-tier stand, which would have increased capacity to 80,000. Newcastle United's plan never got off the drawing board.

And then relationships between club and council dipped to an all time low in the early sixties once United lost the 1966 World Cup attraction due to the inability to secure a development package for St James Park. The World Cup organising committee not unreasonably insisted that substantial improvements had to be made before handing the lucrative stage venue to St James Park. With no decision having been made regarding the club's 1958 proposals, United lodged further plans in 1963 together with a request for a lengthy extension to their lease to protect Newcastle's proposed hefty investment. Meeting after meeting followed, claim and counter-claim bounced around, and headline after headline was created. All that came out of a sorry saga was that the two parties couldn't agree.

The council even drew up their own proposals for a multi-purpose stadium, a 40,000 capacity "Wembley of the North", but the club wanted no part of it. Intermingled into the dispute was a local political Labour v Tory feud as well. There was even talk of the club being evicted from Gallowgate! It was no surprise when the World Cup managers called it a day and handed the stage matches to Middlesbrough instead. Newcastle missed out on the biggest feast of football Britain had seen.

Newcastle United's board was furious. And it was certainly not the end of the affair. For another 20 years the battle over development raged on. After another multi-use sports centre concept was put forward by the Council, the Magpies made serious plans to move from the site. In April 1966 details were revealed of a new arena in Gosforth and by 1968 Newcastle had applied for planning permission. Minister for Sport, Dennis Howell was asked to mediate between the club and landlord, but United pressed ahead with a £1m super-stadium near the racecourse. However, at the last moment in 1971, some semblance of agreement with the Council materialised and the plan was scrapped. A new scheme had at last been agreed for the transformation of St James Park. Yet there was still a long way to go, and many more arguments before redevelopment took shape.

United's stadium just after World War Two, showing the old West Stand and Leazes End Enclosure.

The agreed proposal consisted of four new cantilevered stands all around St James Park, giving an eventual capacity of 47,340. In January 1972 work started on a new Leazes Terrace stand – almost 50 years since the club had first applied for planning permission on that side of the stadium. A year later the stand was opened – even then it appeared to be jinxed and was some months late due to a builder's strike.

It was some time before the next phase started. In 1978, the Leazes End terrace – for so long the favoured haunt of United's fans – was demolished and work started on a cantilevered stand behind the goal. But relegation and recession hit United's finances and there were more problems with the City planners – the Leazes Stand never got out of the ground.

In the aftermath of the Bradford City fire disaster, local councils aimed safety checks on all existing facilities and considering the age of United's West Stand, the Magpies were bound to have problems – and they did. The structure came under vigorous inspection. Newcastle had to start to plan urgently for a replacement.

Another redevelopment proposal was lodged – with the original scheme now scrapped – but the City Council refused permission for the project. Further discussions took place and eventually part of the scheme was accepted. In the close season of 1986 United demolished the 80 year old West Stand and commenced work on an impressive looking £5m structure to become the centre-point of the club's activities. To be named the Milburn Stand as a lasting tribute to Jackie Milburn, it was opened during the 1987-88 season.

Still there was much needed further development of the arena required to take St James Park into the modern era. This however was shelved due to the club's perilous financial position. Newcastle United needed a miracle both on and off the field as the nineties decade opened. That miracle arrived in the shape of Sir John Hall who largely completed a take-over of the club in the opening weeks of 1992.

From that moment everything changed in the fortunes of Newcastle United. And the thorny question of redeveloping St James Park was high on Sir John's agenda. With his experience in property development and his substantial financial backing, a complete new proposal was submitted to the Council for approval. This time Sir John and his team were to reach a quick agreement. The adversity of the past was over. The years of feuding buried. Work started immediately to transform the Gallowgate site at a cost of almost £25m into a stadium to rival any in Britain.

Firstly the Leazes End structure at last rose from the ground. Renamed the Sir John Hall Stand, it was opened for United's debut in the Premiership in 1993. Substantial modifications to the Milburn Stand took place, a new pitch and drainage system installed, new floodlighting as well as the construction of the Gallowgate Stand and infilling all corners of the stadium to produce a marvellous all seater bowl with capacity of around 37,000. Added were impressive corporate and office facilities. Within the space of three short years the new showpiece stadium had been completed. It was a remarkable feat when compared to the previous 70 years of feuding.

Yet the Club still had one major hurdle to overcome. The success of the Magpies warranted a much, much bigger capacity. Newcastle soon needed to expand. Three options were on the table; further develop St James Park, move to another site close by and construction a brand new arena, or move out of the city, to somewhere like Gateshead. A whole new prolific debate was unleashed on the Tyneside

St James Park during Edwardian years.

public. Few supporters wanted to move from their traditional home, while the majority were totally against moving outwith the city boundary.

After much heated debate the club drew up plans for a new 55,000 capacity, £65m stadium to be constructed next door to St James Park in Leazes Park. The existing facilities would be transformed into an indoor arena with extensive parkland between the two centres. It appeared the perfect answer and would have been a great sporting monument for the region to rival Europe's best; the Amsterdam arena, San Siro and Stade de France. But Newcastle United fell into a political quagmire and had to cope with every sort of fringe opposition group with the outcome that the scheme would have to go to Public Enquiry and result in a lengthy delay before commencement – if indeed at all.

Newcastle could not afford to wait. With almost 20,000 paying customers not being able to gain entry to Gallowgate, the club had to reconsider and switch to further developing St James Park. The club's revised proposals to increase the much needed capacity to around 51,000 has been achieved by constructing two huge double tiers to both the Milburn and Leazes Stands at a cost of £42m. After a lengthy – and another controversial planning process – permissions were granted in July 1998 after the Secretary-of-State refused to call-in the application, avoiding the same fate as the Leazes Park development.

The conclusion to a century of development wrangles was finally sealed. With completion due for August 2000, United's new Millennium stadium will be an impressive sight and a landmark for the region.

The Leazes Park development would have given United a brand new stadium.

St James Park at the end of the Millennium, undergoing an expansion to increase capacity to 51,000.

CLUB FILE

YEAR FORMED

As Newcastle East End 1882, as Newcastle United 1892

TURNED PROFESSIONAL

Newcastle East End 1889

LIMITED COMPANY

Newcastle East End 1890

CLUB NICKNAME

The Magpies

GROUNDS

Chillingham Road, Heaton (to 1892),
St James Park (1892 to date)

FOOTBALL LEAGUE RECORD

1893 Elected to Div 2;
1898 -1934 Div 1;
1934 -1948 Div 2;
1948 -1961 Div 1;
1961-1965 Div 2;
1965 -1978 Div 1;
1978 -1984 Div 2;
1984 -1989 Div 1;
1989 -1993 Div 2(1);
1993 - date Premier League.

FOOTBALL LEAGUE CHAMPIONS

1905, 1907, 1909, 1927

PREMIER LEAGUE RUNNERS-UP

1996, 1997

FL DIVISION ONE (TWO) CHAMPIONS
1993

FL DIVISION TWO CHAMPIONS
1965

FL DIVISION TWO PROMOTION
1898, 1948, 1984

FA CUP WINNERS
1910, 1924, 1932, 1951, 1952, 1955

FA CUP RUNNERS-UP
1905, 1906, 1908, 1911, 1974, 1998, 1999

FOOTBALL LEAGUE CUP RUNNERS-UP
1976

FA CHARITY SHIELD WINNERS
1909

FA CHARITY SHIELD RUNNERS-UP
1933, 1952, 1953, 1956, 1996

INTER CITIES FAIRS CUP WINNERS
1969

TEXACO CUP WINNERS
1974, 1975

ANGLO ITALIAN CUP WINNERS
1973

SHERIFF OF LONDON CHARITY SHIELD WINNERS

1907

JAPAN CUP WINNERS

1983

FA YOUTH CUP WINNERS

1962, 1985

EUROPEAN ENTRY

Fairs Cup; 1968-69, 1969-70, 1970-71

UEFA Cup; 1977-78, 1994-95, 1996-97, 1999-2000

Cup Winners Cup; 1998-99

European Champions League; 1997-98

RECORD HOME ATTENDANCE

68,386 v Chelsea, Div One, September 1930

BEST AVERAGE ATTENDANCE

56,299 Div 2 1947-48

RECORD RECEIPTS

£830,270 v Everton, March 1999, FA Cup

RECORD VICTORY

13-0 v Newport County (h), Div Two, October 1946

RECORD DEFEAT

0-9 v Burton Wanderers (a), Div Two, April 1895

RECORD TRANSFER FEE PAID

£15m for Alan Shearer 1996

RECORD TRANSFER FEE RECEIVED

£7.5m for Dietmar Hamann 1999

MOST LEAGUE & CUP GAMES IN A CAREER

496 by J Lawrence 1904-22

MOST LEAGUE & CUP GOALS IN A SEASON

41 by A Cole 1993-94

MOST LEAGUE & CUP GOALS IN A CAREER

200 by J Milburn 1946-57

MOST GOALS IN A LEAGUE & CUP MATCH

6 by L Shackleton v Newport County Oct 1946

MOST CAPPED PLAYER

40 by A McMichael for Northern Ireland 1950-60

OLDEST PLAYER

W Hampson, 42 years 225 days in April 1927

YOUNGEST PLAYER

S Watson, 16 years 223 days in Nov 1990

MANAGERS

Director's Committee 1892-1930;

A Cunningham 1930-35;

T Mather 1935-39;

S Seymour 1939-47 & 1950-54;

G Martin 1947-50;

D Livingstone 1954-56;

Director's Committee 1956-58;

C Mitten 1958-61;

N Smith 1961-62;

J Harvey 1962-75;

G Lee 1975-77;

R Dinnis 1977;

W McGarry 1977-80;

A Cox 1980-84;

J Charlton 1984-85;

W McFaul 1985-88;

J Smith 1988-91;

O Ardiles 1991-92;

K Keegan 1992-97;

K Dalglish 1997-98;

R Gullit 1998-99;

B Robson 1999-

PICTURE GALLERY

Robert Lee, signed by Kevin Keegan for £700,000 and who proceeded to give tremendous service.

One of United's early foreign signings, Brazilian centre-forward Mirandinha.

United's forward line during the thirties: (l-r) Rogers, Livingstone, Smith, Pearson and Mooney.

Newcastle's FA Cup heroes: (Back row l-r) Walker, Hannah, Corbett, Cowell, Batty, Robledo (G), (Front row l-r) Brennan, Stokoe, Fairbrother, Milburn, Crowe and Mitchell.

Newcastle United's welcome home after FA Cup success in 1952.

Silvio Maric, the former Croatia Zagreb star.

Willie McFaul: goalkeeper, coach and manager of the club.

Tony Green, one of Newcastle's talented players during the 1970s.

A goal for Peter Beardsley, congratulated by David Ginola, two key players from Keegan's Entertainers.

Scotland and Newcastle captain, Bob Moncur.

Former England internationalist Stuart Pearce in typical pose.

One of United's greatest-ever players, Peter Beardsley.

A key purchase by Kevin Keegan, ex-Sunderland and Liverpool defender Barry Venison.

Ruud Gullit leads The Magpies out at Wembley in 1999.